AF541590

Social Work
Education and Action

SOCIAL WORK
Education and Action

Edited by
Ranjna K. Devi

OMEGA PUBLICATIONS
NEW DELHI-110 002 (INDIA)

OMEGA PUBLICATIONS
4378/4B, G-4 JMD House
Murari Lal Street, Ansari Road
Daryaganj, New Delhi - 110 002
Phone : 011-23278062,9811787417
e-mail : omega_publications@yahoo.com

© Reserved

Edition : 2023

ISBN : 978-81-8455-186-0

Price : 1295/-

[No part of this publication may be reproduced, Stored in a retrieval system of transmitted, in any form or by any means, mechanical, photocopying, recording or otherwise, without prior written permission of the publisher.]

PRINTED IN INDIA

Published by Mahender Garg for Omega Publications, New Delhi- 110002
Printed at Tarun Offest Press Delhi-110053

Social Work Education and Action

by Ranjna K. Devi

Preface

Social work has a distinguished history of professional involvement in the international community. From its earliest years, for example, the profession: assisted with the resettlement of refugees and other persons displaced by war; operated emergency field relief services for victims of natural and man-made disasters; actively advocated for the rights and protections of disadvantaged and vulnerable population groups; organized groups of oppressed people into effective political entities; and labored to extended programmes of material and social assistance to population groups in need of such services. The fundamental question which Indian social work education is facing today is the same which was asked five decades ago. This relates to its main purpose, objective or goal. In other words, what are students being trained for? Almost every institution of social work education aims at training competent social work personnel for practice in social services and social welfare services. Some institutions even claim that they prepare students for leadership responsibilities in social policy, social planning and social administration; and there are still others which highlight their commitment to social research, scholarly studies and stimulation of public interest in social issues.

Social work education is mainly organised at the master's level because the American model which it copied was primarily at the graduate level till the end of the fifties. Since then institutions for undergraduate social work education in America have multiplied but in India less than a dozen institutions offer the bachelor's degree in social work even today. Just as in America, social work education originated outside the established university education system in India. For many years, most of the institutions functioned independent of any university affiliation. But today almost all of them are either part of the university system or are affiliated to it. Out of nearly 200 Indian universities which cover about five thousand colleges, only nine universities have separate departments of social work, two institutions are deemed to be universities, and all other social work institutions are private colleges affiliated to the university system.

In this study, the following themes are taken here with an elaborate discussion—Social Work Education: An Introductory Overview; Social Work: Scope, Areas & Nature; Social Work Profession: Problems & Issues; Career in Social Work; Strains in American Social Work Education; Women Development Through Government Action; National Plan of Action on Children; Appendices; Bibliography etc.

We are grateful to our publisher for materialising this effort meticulously. We would feel amply rewarded, if comments, constructive criticisms for erudite readers could be communicated to us for enhancement of utility of this project. Comments and suggestions from the users are welcome to enhance it utility, which we may corroborate in subsequent editions. Definitely, the users will find it useful and informative.

—Editor

Contents

	Preface	*v*
1.	Social Work Education: An Introductory Overview	1
2.	Social Work: Scope, Areas & Nature	37
3.	Social Work Profession: Problems & Issues	54
4.	Career in Social Work	100
5.	Strains in American Social Work Education	159
6.	Women Development Through Government Action	184
7.	National Plan of Action on Children	212
	Appendices	248
	Bibliography	273
	Index	276

1

Social Work Education: An Introductory Overview

Social work education is mainly organised at the master's level because the American model which it copied was primarily at the graduate level till the end of the fifties. Since then institutions for undergraduate social work education in America have multiplied but in India less than a dozen institutions offer the bachelor's degree in social work even today. Just as in America, social work education originated outside the established university education system in India. For many years, most of the institutions functioned independent of any university affiliation. But today almost all of them are either part of the university system or are affiliated to it. Out of nearly 200 Indian universities which cover about five thousand colleges, only nine universities have separate departments of social work, two institutions are deemed to be universities, and all other social work institutions are private colleges affiliated to the university system. The pattern of affiliation and management of the twenty-eight institutions shows that nine institutions are under the public management; six are Christian church related and the rest are under other types of private management. The private management of social work education is a question which has rarely been examined or debated as yet. Moreover, the geographical distribution of the existing twenty-eight institutions is also uneven as most states in the north-west and north-east have no social work educational institution.

Professional social workers are generally considered those who hold a professional degree in Social Work. Often these practitioners must also obtain a license or be professionally registered. In many areas of the Western world, social workers start with a Bachelor of Social Work (BA, BSc or BSW) degree. Some countries, such as the United States, also offer post-graduate degrees like the master's degree (MA, MSc or MSW) or the doctoral degree (Ph.D or DSW).

In the United Kingdom, often referred to as social services assistants or care workers, are persons who are not professionally registered and often do not hold any formal social work qualification. In England, to use the term 'social worker', one must register with the General Social Care Council (GSCC). This followed the Care Standards Act 2000 which has protected the title since April 2005 in England. Within the mental health sector in the UK, since November 2008, an additional qualification can be gained: that of an "Approved Mental Health Professional" (AMHP). This replaced the former qualification of "Approved Social Worker" (ASW), and was part of the reform created under the Mental Health Act 2007. This enables the practitioner to assess and make an application to hospital for admission under the Mental Health Act 1983. Whereas previously only qualified social workers could become an ASW, individuals from other qualified professions such as nursing or occupational therapy can also undertake the additional training necessary to be an AMHP. The world of social work looks bright with many promising students at degree level.

In a number of countries and jurisdictions, registration or licensure of people working as social workers is required and there are mandated qualifications. In other places, a professional association sets academic and experiential requirements for admission to membership. The success of these professional bodies' efforts are demonstrated in the fact that these same requirements are recognized by employers as necessary for employment.

In India, professional education for social work began in 1936 when a school of social work was set up in Mumbai by the House of Tatas, one of the largest private industrial and business enterprises. The main inspiration for its establishment came from America partly because its founding Director was an American and partly because the American system of graduate social work education was the only successful model available as compared to other systems elsewhere in some European societies. For eleven years between 1936 and 1947, this Institute was the only one imparting professional education in social work. In 1946, the second institution was established in Lucknow under the auspices of the Young Women Christian Association (YWCA) with a substantial grant from its counterpart in the United States, and again its founder Director was an American. It was shifted to Delhi and was named Delhi School of Social Work. After nearly two years of experimentation, it started a formal two-year programme of social work training in 1949 and was affiliated as a graduate school to the University of Delhi for the Master of Arts degree. This institution was eventually merged with the university in 1979 and became one of its departments for administrative matters under the Faculty of Social Sciences. In 1950, another institution was started as a Faculty of Social Work under the University of Baroda somewhat on the same general pattern of the American model which was accepted earlier at Mumbai and Delhi. During the next decade 1951-60, fourteen more institutions were started in 1971-80. By the end of 1980, thirty institutions were providing social work education and training at the graduate level. It is now reported that the number has grown to fifty or more in the mid-nineties.

This study attempts to look at the Indian social work education and describes its main trends, and assesses the extent to which it has moved toward becoming indigenous in its overall philosophy and goals on the one hand and in terms of the level of training, curriculum content, use of study material and methods of working with people on the other. In the mid-eighties, 28 institutions were requested to send copies of their latest bulletins or prospectuses as they are called; twenty-one sent replies providing them or some other related information while seven failed to supply any information despite several repeated reminders. The material collected from the twenty-one institutions constituted the single most important source of the primary data. Four institutions did not send a separate prospectus. The various volumes of the *Indian Journal of Social Work* were also examined. In addition, informal discussions were held with ten prominent social work educators located in Delhi; five of them worked for the two major institutions of social work; three held important positions with the Government of India; and two were heads of national institutes which were involved in the training of para-professionals or in the organisation of refresher courses for professionals already working in the public and private social welfare organisations.

As a part of this study, an attempt has also been made to determine the extent of international orientation of the American social work education as reflected through the bulletins of several leading schools of social work, the cross-cultural coverage in the volumes of three professional periodicals for the decade 1980-90, and the published study material of the Council on Social Work Education. Finally, the role of the United Nations and its allied agencies in relation to social work education is examined to assess the effectiveness of their international activities in the promotion of indigenous elements in different societies.

Education for Social Work

The main inspiration for the introduction, of the formal training for social work came to this country from the West, especially the United States, when the first training institute was established in 1936 under the directorship of an American. On the eve of Independence in 1947, there were three schools of social work; by 1970, more than twenty schools of social work have been established, of which half of them are reported to be affiliated to the universities, whereas the others function as independent units and award diplomas instead of degrees. All the schools or institutes follow more or less a common pattern of curriculum which usually follows the lines set up by the Tata Institute of Social Sciences which was the pioneering school in the field. The need for professional training as postulated in the bulletins seems to presuppose the existence of a net-work of organised social welfare agencies which are usually to seek the services of persons with such training. Moreover, the bulletins further assume that the type and level of training as offered by the schools of social work are consistent with the requirements of the existing welfare agencies on tie one hand and are in conformity with the cultural values, traditions, and mores on the other. The statistical Study of Social Welfare Agencies aided by the Central Social Welfare Board has shown that out of the 5,000 agencies surveyed, few agencies work in an organised manner, and have any trained person on their staff. This

Study indicates that almost all agencies lack adequate financial resources and can ill-afford to hire trained persons. Some of the voluntary agencies which are located in big cities like Mumbai, Delhi, Calcutta, and Madras, do employ workers who possess the professional training, but they constitute only a fraction in the over-all social welfare system of the country.

Again, neither the type of training nor the level at which this training is offered seems to have met the needs of economic and social development programmes which have been initiated as a part of the Five Year Plans. During the last twenty years, both the Government of India and many state governments have established their own institutes or centres for the training of personnel required for the governmental agencies with the result that few positions become available to those who receive training in the schools of social work. Moreover, as the professional training' for social work is mainly organised at the graduate level and very limited facilities exist for undergraduate training, the scope of employment for persons having the Master's Degree in social work is further reduced. The cultural context also imposes severe limitations on the employment opportunities as the prevailing curriculum in Indian schools of social work is not only based upon the American value system, but is conditioned by American study material, American trained teachers and American field work practices. In recent years some Indian social work educators have commented upon the conflicting nature of social work based on American values and ideology, but practised in Indian society with a different set of values and ethos. As a matter of fact, problems of social work education are increasingly coming to the forefront and the claim adumbrated by the Indian schools of social work that social work profession does exist for which they are training new recruits on a systematic basis is far from reality.

Organisation of Social Work Education

Social work education is mainly organised at the master's level because the American model which it copied was primarily at the graduate level till the end of the sixties. Since then institutions for undergraduate social work education in America have multiplied but in India less than a dozen institutions offer the bachelor's degree in social work even today. Just as in America, social work education originated outside the established university educational system in India.

The history of the New York School of Social Work in New York and thc Tata Institute of Social Sciences in Mumbai presents many similarities in this context. However, in both societies, social work institutions had to seek direct or indirect relationship with their respective university systems in course of time not only to standardise their curricula and improve the quality of training, but also to promote greater acceptance and enhance their status in the academic community.

At present, there are about one hundred graduate schools and several hundred undergraduate programmes in America. In India, out of nearly 200 universities which cover about five thousand colleges, only fifteen universities have separate departments of social work, two institutions are deemed to be universities, and all other social work institutions are only affiliated to universities. The pattern of affiliation and management of the twenty-one institutions included in this study varies. Seven institutions are under public management (four others which did not reply); six are Christian Church related, and the rest are under private management. The private management of social work education is a question which has rarely been discussed or debated as yet.

Major Components of Social Work Education

The programme of education has basically three components: classroom courses, research project and field work. The courses offered are generally divided into four groups. The first group consists of courses about Indian society, social structure, history and philosophy of social work and social problems; the second group relates to the study of human growth and development; and the third group includes courses on methods of working with people such as social casework, social groupwork, community organisation and community development, social welfare administration and social research; and the fourth group is composed of specialised courses usually offered during the second year of training, and students are expected to concentrate on one of them.

The curricula are somewhat similar in all schools, and the original pattern as established by the Tata Institute and the Delhi School in the mid-fifties continues to be followed. But both these institutions had modified their curricula considerably in the late sixties and the early seventies. While at the Tata Institute, most courses continue to be labelled on the American model, the Delhi School has attempted generic terms as methods of working with people instead of the traditional titles as social casework, social groupwork and community organisation. In most other institutions, the traditional terminology is widely followed, and even where new terms have been introduced, the basic teaching material which is primarily American, has remained the same. In addition to the courses, almost all institutions either require or provide opportunities to their students to complete an individual or group research project report based upon some type of field data. Over the years, this requirement has moved from the mandatory level to the optional level especially during the seventies. Without exception, all institutions fully recognise that field work is an integral part of social work training.

The field work programme generally includes concurrent activities, block field placement, study tours and an annual rural camp. During the first year most institutions have observational and unstructured type of field work for about 15 hours a week. The second year field work is somewhat more structured and is usually related to the student's specialised area of interest as chosen at the time of admission. The block field work placement of four to six weeks is generally arranged after the completion of all other formal requirements of training; in two institutions however this is done as a part of the field work during the second year of training. This placement exposes the student to the actual functioning of social welfare agencies and it often leads to his employment as well.

In terms of both emphasis and credit given in the total curricula of different institutions, the field work practices do vary considerably. In general, institutions located in the metropolitan cities of Mumbai, Delhi and Madras have somewhat stronger field work programmes than others. In Baroda where social work constitutes a separate teaching faculty in the university, field work is given the highest credit to the extent of forty per cent in the total curriculum whereas most other institutions assign ten to twenty per cent credit.

In the university system as a whole, the question of giving adequate recognition and credit to the field work proportionate to the time spent by the student has raised a number of problems which fall outside the present discussion. In many institutions especially those established in the seventies and after, field work programmes are somewhat weaker, and in many others, academic courses continue to receive disproportionately higher attention.

Out of the twenty-one institutions covered in this survey, seven have also their own centres or service units for field work training; three did not supply any information while the remaining institutions had no field work centre of their own. The rationale for their establishment is partly based upon the absence of suitable of social welfare agencies and partly because of the non-availability of social work trained supervisors in most field work agencies. Moreover, it has been recognised from time to time that most social welfare agencies cannot relate the use of theoretical knowledge to the social realities in which they normally carry their practice. To overcome these inadequacies, some institutions have therefore justified the establishment and maintenance of service units for providing field work training opportunities to their students.

As a matter of fact, the Tata Institute from its very inception has been maintaining a child guidance clinic for the treatment of personality disorders of children. At present, the Institute also runs a special cell in the office of the Police Commissioner to help women in distress; and there are two additional projects, one to develop job skills among the youth in the slums and the other to help a tribal community in solving some of their basic problems of living. The Delhi School also has a child guidance clinic and a rural development project. Similarly several other institutions are involved directly or indirectly in running community centres, children centres or rural development centres where they place their students for field work training. In such cases, faculty members act both as field work instructors as well as supervisors. This arrangement leads to a considerable burden on the faculty who have to assume day-to-day supervision of students. The effectiveness of such training from service projects has never been evaluated as yet.

Specialities in Social Work Education

The fundamental question which Indian social work education is facing today is the same which was asked five decades ago. This relates to its main purpose, objective or goal. In other words, what are students being trained for? Almost every institution of social work education aims at training competent social work personnel for practice in social services and social welfare services. Some institutions even claim that they prepare students for leadership responsibilities in social policy, social planning and social administration; and there are still others which highlight their commitment to social research, scholarly studios and stimulation of public interest in social issues. But it will not be untrue to say that there are no well defined categories of welfare personnel for which social work training is considered essential at the present time even after about sixty years since the establishment of the first institution. There are however two fields of practice, labelled as medical-psychiatric social work, and personnel management-industrial relations-labour welfare, where social work training is given preference. The former reflects wholesale borrowing from the American social work education model while the latter is an indigenous development because the field of labour welfare has remained outside the traditional social work education in America though industrial social work has taken some roots during the past decade in some institutions located in the metropolitan cities.

During the last three decades, two or three Indian social work educators have justified the creation or the specialisation known as medical and psychiatric social work in their writings. As a field of practice, medical and psychiatric social work is reported to be practised in not more than a few dozen hospitals and clinics in the entire country. Moreover, the subject of psychiatry still remains an unknown entity outside the metropolitan cities numbering about 10 or 12. In a society where the problems of physical health remain massive as reflected in higher rates of infant mortality, maternal mortality, malnutrition and many other forms of morbidity, the establishment and promotion of medical and psychiatric social work seem rather ironic. The teaching of these subjects requires reorientation towards physical health and mental health education.

Moreover, the delivery of medical services on an equitable basis presents yet another serious dilemma which needs more attention of the social work education leadership. The fact that this specialisation has been there for so long is no justification for its continued existence. What is needed instead is health education specialisation incorporating the themes of family planning and planned parenthood taking into consideration the social realities of public health and overpopulation and the overall quality of life. As a matter of fact, most institutions are ill-equipped to train specialists as medical and psychiatric social workers because their training requires high degree of competence on the part of teachers and adequate availability of community resources and agencies for their practice. But both of these conditions are lacking at this time and perhaps will remain so for a long time to come. Among the other specialisations are included, family and child welfare, correctional administration, community organisation and development, tribal welfare and social welfare administration. Most female students are reported to take up family and child welfare and some job opportunities do exist though family social work as it is understood in America is hardly practised except in some agencies in Mumbai. There are great potentialities in correctional administration but in actual practice, social work graduates do not receive any special preference for positions in jails, prisons or courts except in one or two states.

Even in the field of community organisation and community development, social work remains marginal partly because it is primarily in rural communities where community development programmes are functioning and partly because separate institutions exist for the training of rural workers and public administrators. Moreover, community organisation in urban areas has not made much headway though some experiments were launched in the early sixties. The contribution of social work in tribal welfare has been very little so far, though the Tata Institute has been fairly active in offering specialised courses in it during the sixties and the seventies.

Social welfare administration as a specialised field is reported to be available only at three institutes. Perhaps, the Tata Institute is the only one which has somewhat adequate resources and suitable staff to offer this specialisation. Actually, courses on social administration, social policy and social action continue to be the least developed because the main objective of social work education in India as borrowed from America is to train practice-oriented social workers even if there is no market for them. With regard to the specialisation known as labour welfare, personnel management and industrial relations, it should be noted that it happens to be one of the indigenous elements. The original rationale for including this field in social work educational institutions was that the industrial labour was looked upon as an underprivileged group of population which needed special provisions for welfare services in industrial settings through social legislation. Under the Indian Factories Act of 1948 and its various amendments, a beginning was made in this direction and the act required the appointment of labour welfare officers employing two hundred or more workers who were to hold degrees or diplomas in social sciences from any institution recognised by the state government. Both historically and traditionally, the Tata Institute became the initial supplier, and in subsequent years, this specialisation emerged as the most important one for which there was a statutory recognition on the one hand and greater job opportunities on the other.

From time to time, social work educators and social welfare leaders have raised many questions relating to the application of social work philosophy, concepts and theories to this field of specialisation. Moreover, this field itself has kept shifting its emphasis from labour welfare to the activities of personnel management and industrial relations which have come to assume greater importance in the various industrial settings. Again, it was this field of specialisation for which a number of separate training institutions were set up outside the social work education.

Eventually in 1967, the Tata Institute established an independent master's programme in personnel management and industrial relations. Even at the Delhi School, a generic programme was introduced which reduced the importance of all specialisations including the labour welfare. Despite these changes, the specialisation of labour welfare, personnel management and industrial relations continues to remain the most dominant field of study in terms of enrollment, prestige and job opportunities, and this also happens to be the specialisation where there has been an increasing divorce from the established American philosophy, contents and techniques of social work education during the past decade.

Some institutions have even introduced separate diploma or degree courses in this specialisation to compete with the specialised institutions of business and industrial management. How well equipped and effective are social work educational institutions to offer training in the labour welfare specialisation has remained a vexing issue all along. Neither the institutions themselves nor their faculty members have made any serious attempt to integrate social work concepts, theories and techniques with it. The Second Review Committee of Social Work Education of the University Grants Commission had recommended its abolition from social work curricula. Most institutions are however hesitant to accept this recommendation because this specialisation is the only one for which somewhat clear cut job opportunities exist irrespective of the fact whether social work training is actually applicable to the preparation of students for the various responsibilities called for by the employing industrial settings.

Besides, most male applicants who seek out admission to social work training are reported to show preference for this specialisation, and the overall public image of social work continues to be associated with the field of labour welfare. However, the Delhi School which gave up training in formal specialisations several years ago claims to have suffered no loss in its enrollment. The debate on the generic versus specialisation continues, and it is fair to say that most institutions in actual practice tend to emphasise some form of specialisation either at the time of admission of students or in the course of their training during the second year. Moreover, the findings of some studies about the employment of social work graduates have shown that most employers in practice do not maintain any clear distinction between the specialist and the generalist. At the same time, it is noted that most graduates prefer to take up what is available and as more opportunities exist in the specialisation of labour, so its effective demand continues to flourish.

Students and the Faculty

Out of the twenty-one institutions covered by this survey, 15 indicated the available number of seats every year; eight institutions admit 20-35 students; four between 40 and 50; and three more than 50. Among the largest institutions in terms of annual enrollment are the Tata Institute with 70 in its social work programme, the Varanasi School 65; and the Delhi School has 55. Almost all other institutions for which actual data was not available have a capacity of 50 or less each. If the average capacity is taken as forty seats per institution and assuming every one admitted completed his or her training successfully, the annual production of graduates was about 1,100 for a society with a population of about 800 million persons in 1991 and where several thousand organisations both public and private are engaged in some form of social welfare activity.

Ironic as it may sound even one thousand plus graduates cannot find suitable employment because most of these organisations are small and cannot afford to employ professional workers. As a matter of fact, they have failed to accept the useful role of the professionals as such in carrying out their services. There is not much data available about the background of students who join social work education institutions. The Second Review Committee on Social Work Education did make some observations. It was said that students who were drawn to social work education were reported to be those who did not obtain admission to other professional disciplines. It was further pointed out that dead end jobs, lack of commitment of public and voluntary organisations to the need for trained workers, and the subordination of professional workers to volunteers and non-professional committees were responsible for discouraging many students from coming to social work institutions. In addition, the questions of employment opportunities, salary scales, availability of promotions, and acceptance of the professional ethics raised important issues in the recruitment of students. At this stage of economic development. Economics continues to be the only social science which attracts relatively well-prepared students as compared to other social sciences. During the past two decades, the institutions of business management and administration have also been sought after at an increasing rate.

As regards the faculty, it was found that nine out of the seventeen institutions which furnished the necessary data employed less than ten teachers each; four had ten faculty members each; and four had more than fifteen each; and the Tata ranked at the top employing about thirty for its social work programme. Institutions which had undergraduate training programmes also did not show their faculty separately. Many faculty members held double graduate degrees; almost every institution had at least one faculty member with a Ph.D. degree; one-third of the faculty at the Tatas, in Varanasi nineteen out of 20, in Udaipur one-third, and one-fifth in Delhi had doctoral degrees. No data was available about their field experience. Generally speaking, most faculty members had suitable academic qualifications but little or no worthwhile field experience after their graduation. This is consistent with the cultural setting because the Indian academic community continues to give higher rewards for academic achievements, and direct service experience is generally frowned upon historically. The Tata and the Delhi School were the only institutions where 6 or 7 faculty members held American social work degrees; and three other institutions had at least one faculty member each who was an American-trained social worker.

Although the proportion of foreign trained teachers had gone down considerably over the years, the very pattern of organisation and the teaching material used in social work institutions are American both in spirit and content. Most of the faculty lacks research orientation and has published very little except some faculty members at the Tata and the Delhi School who have been fairly productive. But, even they have failed to develop and produce teaching material based upon indigenous social, economic and political conditions. Perhaps, faculty development programmes are needed so that selected faculty members could obtain leave from their teaching duties and work in both public and private social welfare organisations functioning at different levels.

Internationalising Social Work Education

Social work has a distinguished history of professional involvement in the international community. From its earliest years, for example, the profession: assisted with the resettlement of refugees and other persons displaced by war; operated emergency field relief services for victims of natural and man-made disasters; actively advocated for the rights and protections of disadvantaged and vulnerable population groups; organized groups of oppressed people into effective political entities; and labored to extended programmes of material and social assistance to population groups in need of such services. These activities were undertaken at both the national and international levels and, always, with a view toward redressing social injustices where ever they existed in the world.

Social workers also labored on behalf of world peace, an effort that, in time, was to earn for Jane Addams the profession's first Nobel Prize. Since those early years, the profession's international activities have continued to increase and diversify; today, a variety of formal and informal structures exist to channel social work's energies at the international level. Indicators of the importance that the profession attaches to its international activities include:

1. the extraordinary level of private resources that are committed each year in support of international social welfare activities (e.g., from foundations, corporations, community groups, and individuals for support of international programmes of basic education, health care, housing, transportation, and for the development of other welfare-relevant infrastructures);
2. the number, functional diversity, and geographic distribution of international social welfare service organizations (Irvin, 1991);
3. the range and specialized nature of our major international organizations and professional associations, including the International Council on Social Welfare (ICSW), the International Association of Schools of Social Work (IASSW), the International Federation of Social Workers (IFSW), and the Inter-University Consortium for International Social Development (IUCISD);
4. the number and diversity of our specialized journals in international social work, including International Social Work, the Journal of International and Comparative Social Welfare, and Social Development Issues;
5. as reflected in the size of this volume, the

extraordinary body of published materials authored by social workers on international topics of relevance to the profession;

6. the number, frequency, and location of the profession's international meetings and congresses;
7. the existence in many of our national organizations and their local chapters of energetic and forward looking international committees (e.g. in the National Association of Social Workers and the Council on Social Work Education); and
8. the important leadership roles carried by social workers in national and international social development programmes.

The richness of the profession's past and current contributions to advancing human welfare throughout the world is suggestive of the leadership role that the profession will carry as we finish the present century and move toward the beginning of the next—a century in which profound social transformations are expected in virtually all sectors of society, including in social welfare. Most specialists in social development, including social workers engaged in international development, believe that the 21st century will be a "global century," i.e., a century in which the most critical issues on the world agenda will emanate for global rather than national forces. The impact of these worldwide forces on all societal institutions is expected to be enormous and long-lasting. They are expected to result in a significant reshaping of national and international affairs as we know them today.

Among the most dramatic international events that are reshaping our "social futures" are those which are occupying our attention as the present century begins to draw to a close. More than at any other time in human history significant international events are making clear the extraordinary degree of social inter-dependence that exists between people and nations everywhere.

1. The end of the Cold War and, with it, the opportunity to redirect more of the world's resources to life-giving rather than life-taking activity
2. The signing of joint agreements between the United States and the Soviet Union on nuclear and conventional weapons disarmament
3. In response to economic bankruptcy brought on by the arms race and the failure of its central political institutions, the collapse of Communism in the Soviet Union
4. In the Soviet Union, Boris Yeltsin's successful effort to rebuff a conservative political coup that sought to restore totalitarianism to that country
5. Political independence for the Baltic States 6. Political independence and economic autonomy for the nations of Eastern Europe
7. A reunited Germany
8. The economic unification of Europe and, in time, increased social unification as well—especially on welfare issues of special interest to social workers
9. In response to the Iraqi invasion of Kuwait, a revitalization of the United Nation's peace keeping and peace promotion functions
10. The restoration of democracy to the majority of states in Central and South America 11. The beginnings of an Arab-Israeli dialogue on peace
12. Earnest efforts on the part of the United States, Russia, and other member states of the Commonwealth of Independent States to centralize

and, ultimately, to destroy entire classes of nuclear, biological, and chemical weapons

13. The probable reunification of North and South Korea in the near-term

The magnitude of these global events is impressive; they will almost certainly impact on human affairs for decades to come. Their significance, and the rapid pace at which such profound changes are taking place add considerable urgency to international efforts to establish a "new world order," i.e., to work toward the establishment of a new system of international relationships guided by the quest for world peace, increased social justice, the universal satisfaction of basic human needs, and for the protection of the planet's fragile eco-system.

Social Welfare and Social Work in the Modern Time

Though less visible than recent international political and economic events, profound international social changes are also occurring as the present century draws to a close. These changes can be expected to have at least as significant an impact on future world affairs as have recent political and economic changes. Indeed, because of their direct consequences on the daily lives of people, contemporary social trends may prove more long-lasting than those of either a political or economic nature. In either case, significant international social forces already are at work that will profoundly alter patterns of human service delivery in this century. As a result, governments are likely to seek new approaches for dealing with the human services needs of the next century. The need for such approaches will be felt most acutely by welfare leaders in those developing countries in which population growth exceeds their capacity to satisfy even basic needs.

Ultimately, acting in cooperation with their

governments, social welfare specialists will need to give leadership to the development of new public/private partnerships in the provision of human services. These partnerships will need to include both traditional providers of human services as well as new actors in the welfare enterprise. In general, social welfare partnerships of the future will almost certainly reflect significantly enlarged roles for "non-governmental organizations," business and other commercial enterprises, community organizations, religious institutions, volunteers, mutual aid societies, self-help groups, unions, consumer protection associations, colleges and universities, in addition to representatives of mass communications media. Significantly expanded systems of special support for families, family systems, and age-dependent persons living outside of families will also need to be major components of any reorganized social welfare system.

The social work profession—because of its unique history, knowledge, value, and skill base—is particularly qualified to provide leadership on these critical international issues. Certainly, social workers of the future will continue to occupy significant national and international leadership positions. Their task, as was that of past generations, will be to find innovative solutions to the social welfare problems that confront their generation. Subtitled "A Guide to Resources For a New Century," this book is dedicated to those emerging social work leaders on whose shoulders fall the responsibility of preparing for a new century.

UN Role

During the past four decades, the United Nations and its many commissions and allied agencies have also played a role in the dissemination of American social work in other countries. The United Nations brought out five surveys which identified significant developments and trends in the training programmes in social work in different countries. The surveys, specifically the third and the fourth, highlighted the limited applicability of the American model of social work education and pointed out the need for promoting indigenous methods, curricula and study material. In subsequent years, the United Nations Commission in Bangkok took several initiatives dating back to 1964 to promote the development of indigenous teaching material by establishing a working group consisting of well-known social work educators from the South Asian region.

Moreover, the Commission also sponsored a training centre in September 1966 which offered social work teachers an opportunity to work together jointly so as to identify the main principles of curriculum on an indigenous basis, to incorporate cultural factors in the practice of social work and to develop teaching material including case studies reflecting socio-economic conditions of the region. In later years, the United Nations Centre for Social Welfare and Development in Manila held many conferences and seminars involving selected representatives of schools of social work for mutual exchange of views on issues and problems, and for the development of indigenous case records and other teaching material. It is true that based upon the proceedings of these conferences and seminars, several surveys and reports became available stressing the importance of the development of indigenous approaches and study material. But it is unfortunate that neither any concrete plan has been developed to replace the American model nor any specific indigenous study material has been produced during the past two decades. This may be partly attributed to the fact that most of the United Nations publications and personnel tacitly have assumed all along that American social work philosophy is somewhat superior, and that principles and methods of American social work provide the only model which has universal applicability.

Need for Indigenous Foundations

The need for indigenous elements of social work education in terms of its philosophy, approaches, principles, theories and study material cannot be over-emphasised because working with people, studying social problems and administering social welfare programmes call for indigenous orientation and skills. The foreignness of social work education is so much all-inclusive and pervasive as reflected in its basic organisation, curricula and the teaching material that most social work graduates fail to pursue careers in professional social work. Moreover, existing training does not prepare them to assume roles of leadership in the planning, formulation and implementation of social welfare programmes at different levels of practice and administration. If social work has to move toward professionalism in any society and has to become effective, it must have indigenous foundations incorporating dominant cultural philosophies, on the one hand, and projected goals which are being promoted on the other.

Recently, based upon his independent study, a young Indian social educator has concluded that "social work education in India has become irrelevant to the needs of Indian society, because what is needed in Indian society is a primarily preventive and macro based social work." Indian social work educators must accept this challenge and forge a new strategy to transform the existing social work education to develop and use indigenous study material. Unless this is done social work as a profession is not likely to establish its roots in society.

Rethinking Social Work Education

The first step in the process of rethinking is the bringing to consciousness the model or models that dominate our thought and action, the second task is to analyse the model itself to accept, modify or reject it and lastly to construct a new model/or models if need be. An overview of the writings of people who initiated social work education in India reveals that they were faced with the dilemma of choosing a specific model designed to meet the requirements of Indian conditions.

Clifford Manshardt, the initiator and director of the first school of social work in Asia, was aware that it was "quite impossible to reproduce Western experience without first submitting it to a great amount of critical analyses and scrutinizing each subject in the light of Indian conditions" (Manshardt, 1941). Dr. Holt in his address at the opening of the first graduate school in 1937 emphasised the value of the experience Manshardt and his colleagues had in actually working with people, as also their desire to establish it on indigenous lines. "It would be easy to take the ideas of modern social work from the West and found a school for its propagation and the adventure would probably be as dangerous as it would be useless. But it is a different matter to relate such a school to the experience of 10 years of actual living in Byculla, challenged by every problem with which human nature is puzzled (Manshardt, 1941). Although Manshardt introduced a theoretical and methodological orientation in some respects similar to that of the USA yet he emphasised that "the School recognises that the cultural, economic and social conditions of India differ from those of the West and it makes every effort to adopt its materials to Indian conditions to interpret them in the light of the national and social heritage" (Marshartd, 1941).

Some of the goals identified by Titus, apart from the conventional goals of helping people or remedial services were (i) to alter the environment in such manner as to make it more suitable for those who cannot under existing circumstances maintain themselves economically (ii) to improve standards of living in general by means of a more equitable distribution of wealth (iii) to facilitate and implement social change on one or all of the following levels (a) increased institutional flexibility in terms of changing human needs (b) increased central emphasis (social values) in relation to civilisation (technology) (c) enhanced opportunities for progressively minded individuals to function without restraints (d) destruction of the existing socio-economic order by constitutional or revolutionary means in order to make way for a socialised state (Titus, 1941).

The adoption of the curative and rehabilitative goals over the goals which emphasised change perhaps can be explained by (i) a long tradition of welfare services based on the theory of individual inadequacy and fatalism (ii) the philosophical orientation of Manshardt and others involved in the delivery of services (iii) the models of social work available as reference points (iv) the lack of empirical evidence pertaining to the ineffectiveness of welfare services particularly in dealing with the problem of poverty (v) and finally the lack of theoretical insights about the problems of the developing countries. To this now may be added the 'market forces' i.e. the market for goods produced by the schools of social work. The biggest consumers of products of schools of social work are large commercial organisations, governmental institutions and non-governmental institutions largely funded by government or international sources informed by a liberal ideology of social welfare. The dilemma of choosing a specific model of social work education still haunts some, though in practice the schools have continued in the same vein almost oblivious of the whole controversy.

The objectives of professional education currently are to prepare the type and quality of manpower capable of performing the professional tasks and functions currently being performed by a variety of organisations employing social workers.

Main Tasks and Functions of Social Work

The report of the second review committee appointed by the University Grants Commission, to review social work education identified two 'categories of social work tasks (a) developmental and (b) remedial and rehabilitative (U.G.C. 1980).

The major goal of social work was seen as to enhance the well being of people to ensure social justice and opportunity for people to develop their capacities to become participating and contributing citizens. There is however, hardly any agreement on what the term 'development' stands for. For example Nafisa considers the problem of poverty as a systemic problem and not an is dated problem. "It is related to socio-economic structures at every level; to decision making patterns in society, in terms of who takes decisions, for whom and how?, and it is related to the model of development that we have chosen to adopt in our country which is based on the principle of elitism.

Hence it is in this context that we must understand the goals of social change (Nafisa, 1984). Keeping the social realities in mind the goals of social change must aim to deal with the status of the poverty groups in society.

More specifically to develop their capacity to participate in decisions that affect them in the social, economic and political spheres. This would imply efforts to develop people's organisations and movements at the grass root level, develop people' bargaining power, develop their economic capacity so that they may be involved in problem solving; developing their functional skills so that it can enhance their participation in decisions that affect them. Social change must then imply fundamental changes which Arthur Dunham terms as relationship goals in community organisation i.e. basically changing relationship patterns between landlords and labourers, industrialists and employees, slum dwellers and government etc. Secondly, given the institutional context we need to bring about a change in terms of the policy framework and institutional functioning so that they are more relevant to the client system they serve.

Basically this would mean a change in delivery of service to ensure that the right people got the right services. Historically, the main concern of the social work profession has been to work within the institutions. It is important to work towards institutional relevance as there is a divergence between community needs and institutional functions. For example, this is most evident in the area of health where the hospital as an institution does not necessarily serve the health needs of the community. Just as the school does not necessarily cater to the educational needs of a majority of our children in poverty groups, as correctional institutions for children do not necessarily cater to the emotional needs of neglected children"' (Nafisa, 1984).

Yet another view of development provided by Kulkarni is (i) a policy of distributive justice to reshape the strategy focussed earlier exclusively on increased production; (ii) a policy of purposeful institutional change to match with modernisation of technology; (iii) a policy of employment promotion with a priority at least equal to, if not higher than that of the growth of the GNP; (iv) a policy of development of human resources; (v) a policy of people's participation in development planning" (Kulkarni, 1979). A third view of developmental social work termed it as "policy practice". The social workers begin their interventions by talking with collateral systems about a population at risk. This criterion seem relatively-straightforward in categorizing a city welfare administrator, for example, who consults with staff and city council members in formulating policy about processing welfare applicants. Although considerably less straightforward, a social work researcher would also be classified as a policy practitioner insofar as the focus would be on, formulating a study to draw inferences about future clients, that is, populations-at-risk" (Jackson, et. al., 1984).

The word 'Political' is understood here to mean a collective decision making process of the group and the knowledge and organisational power involved among the people at grass root level. This should not be confused with party's political power. In this framework, political power will not and should not be an end in itself. It is expected to lead to further growth towards liberation of self and society" (Ramachandran, 1986).

"The goal of developmental social welfare is primarily to meet the basic needs of the large majority of the people who live and work in dehumanising conditions, and progressively to work towards the improvement in the quality of their lives.... The concept of social development will vary to some extent according to the present situation of the country.... whatever may be the concrete expression of the constituent elements of such a society and the means to achieve it, it will necessitate significant changes at the organisational, institutional and social structural levels (Pathak, 1981).

The UGC report referred to the Vth International Survey for training in social welfare in identifying the developmental tasks (UN, 1971). These developmental tasks were seen to be related to work with specific target groups where social functioning is of crucial concern to social welfare. Ensuring interdisciplinary delivery of services, providing opportunities for the involvement of communities in problem solving and bringing about change in institutional structure or processes which retard, block or deflect development, were the specific tasks mentioned (UGC, 1980).

Pinkus and Minahan have formulated seven tasks for social work which they define as planned change effort. The seven tasks stated by Pinkus and Minahan (1973) can broadly be grouped into four functions:

(i) to enable the people to cope with their problems by making use of their own capacities and resources;

(ii) to act as mediator between people with needs and the resources provided by the society. This includes also the tasks of facilitating people's access to the resource system and influencing them to be more responsive to the needs of the people;

(iii) the provision of concrete material goods and services which is termed by the authors as the task of dispenser of material goods and services;

(iv) contributing to the formulation and modification of social policies. (Pinkus & Minahan, 1973).

The similarity between the tasks and functions identified by UGC report and Pinkus and Minahan is obvious. As Pathak pointed out "It is interesting to note that despite their emphasis on planned change efforts, in their statement of tasks there is none that directly and obviously deals with the role of an agent of social change. Wilson's critique of ideology and welfare sums up the linkage between social change and social work, and their periodic efforts to adopt new models and techniques. "The ideology of the welfare state expresses itself above all in what is written about social work and social workers, the literature of social work is the ideology of welfare capitalism..... This literature is not-or certainly, not always—overtly reactionary or conservative, rather it fetishizes change and innovation, as happens also in the productive process where new models constantly replace old (yet the new models are always essentially the same as the old. Pincus and Minhan's book (1973) is an especially delicious example of old wine in new bottles, with a new jargon to describe the old activities).

The latest word for social workers is indeed 'change agent'. Just as modern capitalism and social democracy constantly attempt to incorporate revolutionary capitalists so social work is ever fetishizing some new methods of work in order to evade the crucial issue of what its function is" (Wilson 1977). It is generally not realised that the 'professional goals' of social work in preparing students to undertake jobs in various fields of social welfare, and the task of bringing about social change in society, particularly when it means disturbing the status quo, contradict each other. The relationship between social work and social policy is determined by the latter, which has its base in the political ideology of the state. Social Work, then, inevitably becomes one of the institutions for legitimizing the political ideology of the state as is the case with education. The choice of a paradigm would require an interpretation of the data on social conditions.

Gradual progress and a hope for better achievements in future based on higher economic growth rates and lower population growth. Social work in that context would need to concentrate on reorganizing its educational programmes to develop better professional skills among the students and further making efforts to prevent them from developing any doubts either about the underlying ideological assumptions or its practice. A radical perspective of social work on the other hand, would require delinking social work education from the state sponsorship followed by the promotion of voluntary organisations committed to the philosophy of change, to carry out both social work education and practice. The choice of a model of society to ensure equality of access to developmental facilities and benefits has to be consciously made along with non-violent viable strategies for the transformation of the present societies. The social work education in this context would concentrate more on developing methodological sophsitication and skills designed to affecting 'change' rather than the delivery of services.

This bring us back to the problem of determining the specific objective of social work education. Can the remedial or clinical model be combined with developmental model? Or, would it be better to focus on any one model? If a competency based education is to be imparted the choice of a single model on the part of the students would be obvious to develop specific skills knowledge and attitudes related to a specific model. The clinical model will focus primarily on the use of social work intervention at micro and meso level, covering a wide variety of settings. A developmental model or system change model would exclusively focus on social work intervention at macro level. Designing separate courses with specific objectives seems to be the only way of solving the present dilemma of 'social' vs the 'professional' (Siddiqui, 1984) or 'personal' vs the 'political' (Halmos, 1970). Development of separate courses on Social Policy in the Schools of Social Work in Canada, USA, UK and New Zealand is reflective of the new trend. In the Indian context the current practice in different schools seems to reflect the assumption that the two models could be combined, for all students.

The UGC report and more recently the participants at a meeting of social work educators to discuss the curriculum outline at TISS Mumbai, endorsed this view. The rationale was that social work practice should be seen as a continuum from micro to macro level, and hence the curriculum should be designed keeping in view the traditional/remedial and promotional/developmental/system change roles'. The micro-macro approach means dealing with a vast range of situations ranging from individual problems of malfunctioning to change of oppressive and unjust systems. The theoretical understanding required for such wide ranging tasks could easily be comprehended. Can this be achieved given the present resources in terms of time, faculty position, quality of field instructors, library facilities, current teaching methodologies, laboratory and field practicum opportunities and lastly the student motivation and capacities to acquire both? To quote Gore, 'If we really want to take on broad social developmental tasks as part of our professional responsibilities, our curricular content in social science will have to be wider and deeper. Our knowledge in the areas of developmental economics organisational behaviour and the analysis of social systems will have to be extended at least to the extent to which we emphasise the understanding of human motivation, psychological processes and abnormal psychology in preparing psychiatric social workers- Is this a realistic goal for our schools? Can this be attempted in a two year programme of instruction where we admit students even without any base in social sciences? (Gore, 1981).

To conclude therefore a competency based model for social work education must begin with identifying specific tasks, and develop a suitable theoretical framework for performing these tasks. It is obvious that the segmental affiliations of social work educators have become complex in recent years. While these divisions are not clear cut, it is clear that there is considerable disagreement and conflict over the nature of social work education. This poses difficulties of defining in any precise way the skills and knowledge relevant for competent social work practice. The micro to macro continuum therefore is bound to create uncertainty on the part of both the educators and the learners. Hence the two should be kept separate if a competency based education is the objective; to enhance the professional status of social work.

REFERENCES

Eugene Pusic, *Reappraisal of the United Nations Social Programmes,* (New York, 1965).

G.R. Banerjee of Tata and Professor K.D. Gangrade have made some attempts to integrate selected indigenous elements in their publications on social casework and community organisation respectively.

Gore M.S. 1981: The Scope of Social work Practice" in T.K. Nair (ed.), Social Work Education and Social Work Practices in India Madras, Association of Schools of Schools of Social Work in India.

Government of India, University Grants Commission, *The First Review Committee for Social Work Education,* (New Delhi, 1965) and *Review of Social Work Education in India: Retrospect and Prospect. Report of the Second Review Committee,* (New Delhi, 1978).

Halmos, P. 1978: *The Personal and the Political,* London, Hutchinson.

Hans Nagpaul, *Culture, Education, and Social Welfare, Need for Indigenous Foundations,* (New Delhi, S. Chand, 1979).

Helen Wright, "Similarities and Differences in Social Work Education as Seen in India and North America," *International Social Work,* January, 1959.

Herbert Aptaker, "Social Work in Cross Cultural Perspective;" in S.K. Khinduka (ed.) Social *Work in India,* (Allahabad, 1965).

Jackson C Eugene, Macy J. Harry Day J. Phyllis 1984: *"A Simultaneity Model for Social Work Education".*

K.S. Mandal, "American Influence on Social Work Education in India and its Impact", *International Social Work,* 1989, Vol. 32; also see, Krishnan Nair (ed.). *Social Work Education and Social Work Practice in India,* op.cit.

Kulkarni, P.D. 1979: *Social Policy and Social Development in India,* Madras, Association of Schools of Social Work in India.

Lee James Midgley, *Professional Imperialism* (London, Heinemann, 1981). No Western scholar has ever written such a forceful critique of American social work and its global diffusion.

Mans Shardt, Clifford 1971: "Education for Social Work," *Indian Journal of Social Work.* Vol. II, No.1.

Nafisa D'Souza 1984: *Social work Education:- A Prospective for Social Change,* Mumbai Mimeographed.

Pathak Shankar 1981: *Social Welfare,* Delhi. MacMillan India Ltd.

Pincus, A. & Minahan, Anne 1973: *Social Work Practice: Model and Method.* Ithaca: Peacock Publishers.

Ramachandran P. 1986: *Perspective for Social Work Training 2000 A.D.* Mumbai, Mimeographed.

Richard J. Estate, "Social Work Research Centres, in *Social Work Research and Abstracts,* Vol. 15, November 2,1979.

Siddiqui H.Y. (ed) 1984: *Social Work and Social Action,* New Delhi, Harnam Publication.

T. Krishnan Nair (ed.) *Social Work Education and Social Work Practice in India,* (Madras, Association of Schools of Social Work in India, 1981).

Titus P.M. 1941: The Place of Research in Social Work" *Indian Journal of Social Work,* Vol. 11, No.1.

Turner, F.J. 1974: *Social Treatment.* New York. The Free Press.

Wilson, Elizabeth 1977: *Women and the Welfare State,* London, Tavistock Publication.

2

Social Work: Scope, Areas & Nature

> "Social work practice is recognised by a constellation of values, purpose, knowledge and interventive techniques. Some social work practice shows more extensive use atone or the other of the components. but it is social work practice only when they are all present to some degree".
>
> *—Harriett Barlett*
> *Encyclopaedia of Social Work*

Scope

Any discussion on the basic concepts of social work create some questions in mind. One of those important questions is identifying the areas where social work should intervene. This question includes many questions in it, such as:

1. In which area social work should intervene? It is difficult to ascertain because almost all the people from all the walks of life need some help occasionally or continuously.
2. Should the help be available at the door step or should the client have to ask for if?

3. Should social work be used in smallest quantity or should it be a natural part of the social structure and Social system? Should social work develop and grow along with the social needs.
4. What is the special role of social work profession when in every area help is provided to the needy by various categories of the professionals such as teachers, doctors, advocates, nurses, bus conductors, bankers, army personnel and priests. Amidst all of them what special role do social workers play in the social system?

No thinking on the above mentioned issues would start unless we fully understand what is social work and what is its role. It is difficult to define as to what social work is, but it is much more difficult to understand what social work is not.

The nature of social work is ambiguous. Therefore It is difficult to be defined and to ascertain scope of social work is also equally difficult. But for knowing boundaries of social work we should try to develop a clear concept of the nature and scope of social work in order to understand rationale of the areas of social work practice. The areas of social work practice basically depend on the scope and nature of social work.

Let us see what all is included in social work. As it has been said by Nitto and Neece quoting NASW "Social work is a professional activity of helping individuals, groups or communities enhance or restore their capacities for social functioning and creating societal conditions favourable to this goal. Social work practice consists of the professional application of social work, values, principles and techniques to one or more of the following ends.

- Helping people obtain tangible services.
- Counselling and psychotherapy with individuals families and groups.
- Helping communities or groups provide social and health services.
- Participating in relevant legislative processes.

This is a detailed self explanatory definition but still they further say that main problem has been due to two approaches.

(i) Direct intervention efforts to help individuals.

(ii) Efforts to accomplish institutional and policy changes to provide indirect help. They believe that there are so many diversities but the profession is integrated on the basis of values which are almost common.

Another definition is given by Baer and Federico here social work is explained in a different dimension. "Social work is a profession concerned with the relationship between people and their environments that affect the ability of people to accomplish life task, realise aspiration and values and alleviate distress".I other words Baer and Federico feel that all these efforts are basically to establish a deeper or better relationship between people and their natural, social, political and economic environment. It means that they want to take social work in a broader perspective.

Here comes a question that all the public dealing professionals are helping people, then what is so different about social work. For finding answer we will have to analyse it. It is a helping profession but that is so in the case of medicine, nursing, low and police etc. The definition clarifies the essential components of social work such as, knowledge, values, purpose and skills. This makes the task easier for us to determine the boundaries of social work practice. But some basic, if subjective, concepts like improvement. betterment and development again make the profession of social work a little vague. "In simplest terms social workers help people improve their interaction with various aspects of their world their children, parents, spouse, family, friends, co-workers or even organisations and whole community. Social work is a profession committed to improving the quality of life for people through various activities directed towards social change". This shows that social work is a little different form other professions because it takes up the function of relating people to the various aspects of their environment and to improve the quality of life by changing and improving society. Before developing any final opinion about the areas of social work let us try to examine the objectives and functions of social work. There has been a lot of subjectivity associated with social work theory and practice. To settle the controversy about social work practice, working statement of National Association of Social Work may be taken as a frame of reference. In 1979 they had declared.

> "The purpose of social work is to promote or restore a mutually beneficial interaction between individuals and society in order to improve the quality of life for every one".

> "Transactions between individuals and others in their environment should enhance the dignity individuality and self determination of every one. People should be treated humanely and with justice".

While discussing the objectives they hove declared "Social workers focus on person and environment in interaction. To corry out their purpose, they work with people to achieve the following objectives:

- Help people to enlarge their competence and increase their problem solving and coping abilities.
- Help people to obtain resources.
- Make organisations responsive to people.
- Facilitate Interaction between individuals and others in their environment.
- Influence interactions between organisations and institutions.
- Influence social and environmental policy.

To achieve these objectives, social workers work with other people. At different times, the target of change varies it may be the client, others wise it is the environment or both". Functions and objectives of social work give us an idea about areas and fields of social work.

Nature of Social Work Assistance

The problem of residual and developmental approach to social work has created a drift among thinkers and philosophers of social work thinkers are in a dilemma. As M.S. Gore has discussed "... whether we should seek to incorporate the whole area of social development within the exclusive domain of social work practice? My own answer is in the negative. I think the distinguishing characteristic of social work lies not in its social science know how ... but in its concern for those in need of help — the deprived, the underprivileged, the unadjusted and the handicapped".

But contrary to this S.H. Pathak has said "... another section strongly differs from this view advocating a radical stance by social workers with reference to the issues of social injustice exploitation and oppression (including gender related discrimination and oppression). The latter group includes those whose ideology ranges from Freire's conscientisation to pro Marxist ideologies that aim to bring about a major social structural change not excluding confrontation and conflict as part of their strategies ... A majority of social work educators are highly sceptical of our legitimacy and competence to prepare social workers for the radical, confrontationist practice in the field".

It is evident with the above discussion that it is not only nature of social work assistance but also definition and scope of social work which will determine the areas for social work intervention. To make it simple one can say that in residual and clinical social work the help is a pain killer tablet but in developmental social work the help is like nutrition and regular health check up which will improve the health so much that pain killer tablet may not be required.

Role of Social Worker

Basically social worker are working to enhance social functioning. As it has been said "During the history of social work many attempts hove been made to describe its nature and purpose and to differentiate social work from other helping professions. The curriculum study of 1955 determined social functioning to be a central purpose of social work and 'intervention' was seen as the enhancement of social functioning.

With this back-ground now we can understand the much used definition in a better way. "Social work seeks to enhance social functioning of individuals singly and in groups by activities focused upon their social relationship which constitute the interaction between man and environment. These activities can be grouped into three categories such as restoration of impaired capacity, provision of individual and social resources and prevention of social dysfunction." These are the broad categories of functions performed by the social workers. Almost all the broad categories fall in these three groups.

One can very well visualise that according to the expected role of the social worker we can divide the areas (it can be vice-versa too). One more point is also clear that some other professionals are also working in similar areas. We will consider the specifications of social work approach which will make social work distinct from other professions. In fact social workers acquire general skills which can be useful in all the fields because we cannot provide specialisation according to areas or fields.

New areas and new fields are getting merged in social work scenario. As Morales and Sheafor have said "one factor that makes social work different from many other professions is the opportunity to engage in helping people deal with a wide range of human problem without needing to obtain specialised professional credentials for each area of practice. In this whole discussion the most important issue is to identify distinct role of the social worker but before that we should examine what are the other professions doing with similar problems.

First of all, the profession with similar boundaries is psychiatry and counselling. Some technical terms, activities and procedures are common though they are as similar to social work as twin sisters who look alike but are different individuals Skidmore has remarked while comparing social work and psychiatry. "Psychiatry tends to focus on pathology and the healing of illness, social work concentrates on strength and the development of potential. The psychiatrist is particularly interested in the internal dynamics of individual and group behaviour. The social worker is specially concerned about social functioning involving social and community factors and interaction". Secondly, nursing and some jobs of para-medical staff look quite similar to social work but there are major differences on the basis of approach, skills and purpose. This difference keeps them distinct. Public administration and town planning are two other professions which are in the disguise of social work. Social welfare administration is quite close to public administration.

Both public administrator and town planning experts look after the needs of slum dwellers poor and needy. It is possible that some social workers are working in various town planning departments but social workers are more concerned with the human factor whereas public administration and town planning professions are working more for the physical features of the area. This way, there is no overlapping as far as role of social worker is concerned.

Types of Users and Clients for Social Work Services

The classification of social work fields might be on the basis of type of clientele. This state may even look absurd become usually it should be the other way that means first we select the fields then automatically those who need welfare services in those fields because the clients for them who are working in those areas but sometimes it happens that those who are poor, needy and who cannot help themselves, are dissatisfied with the situations around, become the client and it is for the social worker to find what type of services do they need. Usually they need all sort of supportive services.

Features of Social Work Intervention

Now let us see what are those distinct features which

make social work intervention a unique type of assistance aiming towards enhancing social functioning.

- Most common distinct feature is the approach of self-help and mutual help. In social work self-help is the most important point in the action plan. In group work and community organisation the concept of mutual help is used to mobilise group or community resources. This approach is by and large absent in the other professions.
- Second distinct feature is the constructive and purposeful use of 'self' which creates professional relationship. Use of the personal qualities and individual uniqueness of the worker is much more meaningful for social work. It has some importance in other professions but professional self and professional relationships are distinct feature of social work only. Relationship is the key for mobilising human factor.
- Third feature is social work's respect for individuality and its uniqueness. Here it is worth mentioning that a social worker perceives individuality in groups and communities also because they have their own uniqueness. This uniqueness makes generalisation difficult. Consequently instead of having any ready-made formula of treatment or betterment social work educators want to develop professional self of the worker so that he can help the client with basic insight and experience.
- Social work cares a lot about the small groups and face to face relationship. For them family is the most important small group. In Indian context we still have strong family ties which absorb so many hardships of social life and preserve the basic equilibrium of its members. Social work profession

not only wants to preserve family but also works to strengthen it.

- Ideal of utilising available resources is another feature of social work practice. Mobilising community resources, government assistance, pressure groups and public opinion are the common processes in social work practice. Identifying client's talents and developing them also comes under the same category.
- Basically, social work has an optimistic approach. It believes in the basic worth and dignity of every human being. It works for the happiness and satisfaction of human beings. It does not propagate self denial and extreme of sacrifice which might create nothing but frustration. It believes that human sufferings can and should be eliminated. They should not be considered indispensable.
- Professional social work needs classroom instructions and field work experience. Supervision and guidance are the tools for developing professional self capable of creating professional relationship. Its training is a process of sensitisation and desensitisation both. Sensitisation for the misery and deprivation and desensitisation for the condition in which worker works. It does not mean that social worker are trained to take these uncomfortable conditions as tolerable situations. They are desensitised only to the extent that worker should not refuse to work in those situations.
- Social work has taken much from psychiatry, psychology and sociology. Besides them it is also indebted to Public Administration, Law. Economic, Political Science and International affairs which provide knowledge base for social work but social

work uses this knowledge for practical work and not for the sake of theory only.

- Social work believes in the establishment and arrangement of the units (institutions) of society such as family, school, government institutions, church or other religious institutions etc. It does not propagate in favour of overnight change. It always prefers slow process of change which is genuinely accepted by people because social workers always want to preserve the client's right of self determination.
- Social work prefers a team approach. The team works with psychiatrists, doctors, probationary officers, police, family planning workers, counsellors and many other professionals. All other professionals work with the problem or need but social worker works with the individual group or community as a whole.
- When we come to the methods and techniques we feel that some methods are used by social worker only, though similar methods and techniques are used by other professionals but this similarity is only superficial. Case work is social work method but similar method is used by counsellors and psychotherapists etc.; group work is a part of social work but a similar activity is used by sports instructor and games incharge etc. Community organisation method is used sometimes by social activists and political leaders. In all these cases when these methods are used by social workers there is a difference in the approach, philosophy and objectives.
- The main objective of social work activities is awareness generation because of the right of self

determination social worker cannot compel any one to follow his suggested alternatives. Therefore basically social worker tries to develop right mindedness among the clients.

- Social work also provides services and material free of cost Sometimes it looks that it is nothing but organised charity which is required in India. It is not against the concept of self-help because certain basic things must be provided by welfare state irrespective of any one's contribution to the society. Here comes another question: do we want trained social workers for working in all social services and social welfare fields such as income maintenance, child survival, nutrition and old age pension schemes? If yes, then are they social work practice areas? If no, then are they some other profession's practice areas? In the developed western countries they are part of state social welfare or social security programmes. In India also state is involved in all such programmes and no body has any clear idea about the human resources available for them. Mostly the salary of the workers in these programmes is so low that whosoever is available, gets absorbed. In the real sense we need paraprofessionals for it.

In the end, one must understand that the areas of social work might be fixed on the basis of residual and developmental social work. Wilensky and Lebeaure's concepts about the model of social welfare may be quoted, "Two conceptions of social welfare seem to be dominant in the United States today : the residual and the institutional. The first holds that social welfare institutions should come into play when the normal structure of supply, the family and the market break down. The second contrast sees the welfare services as normal 'first line' function of modern industrial society". For seven decades social workers have followed the traditional and residual model but offer that another dimension emerged which has also broadened the areas.

Developmental approach in social welfare points out the approach of institutional change. It is basically preventive in nature. P.D. Kulkarni has classified this prevention into three categories. Primary, secondary and tertiary. The first type of prevention is for those who are at the verge of getting involved with the problem. Secondary is for those who do not have any problem for the time being but are from vulnerable group. Tertiary prevention includes those preparatory activities which aim towards long term planning and general well being. Here surfaces a question.

After all what is exactly meant by social development? Developmental social work is a broad based macro level approach to social work where the worker also shares the fruits of social development just like his client. In other words the boundary line between social worker and the client does not exist so distinctly in social development e.g. when we work against corruption or communal tension we are trying to help everyone around including our own selves. As it has been said "Developmental social work Is a crusade which needs total involvement, total planning and policy making. As developmental workers, social workers have to work more as social activists .... social development is basically a planned, directed and desired movement for quick change in the society". With this explanation we now realise that developmental social work is not always in favour of establishment or statusquo. However, let us now examine how residual and developmental models influence the areas and fields of social work today.

Residual or Traditional Social Work Takes Care of

a. Children
b. Handicapped
c. Sick and injured
d. Aged and infirm
e. Drug addict
f. Women in distress
g. Scheduled caste and scheduled tribes
h. Victims of crime
i. Delinquents and criminals
j. Illiterates
k. Needy and deprived
l. Victims of natural and social calamities

Developmental and Preventive Social Work Deals with

a. Community organisation
b. Social action against social problems
c. Child survival
d. Women's empowerment
e. Youth welfare and development
f. Family welfare planning
g. Commuenaltension
h. Rural and urban poverty
i. Slum improvement
j. Vagrancy and truancy
k. Ecological balance
l. Consumers protection
m. Global issues such as human right protection

In short, it is quite obvious from the above discussion that in the same/similar areas many other professionals are also working, therefore it is not 'area' but the approach and mode of assistance which make social work intervention a social work activity. This is important for us to note that these areas cannot be devided in watertight compartments. Many areas provide opportunity to work in both developmental and residual fields.

Service Giving Bodies: Resources & Capacity

Every society develops its own network of services with or without the support of state. Needs are always growing but resources are incompatible to them. Therefore any planned programme of social work and social welfare will have to be based on priorities and capacity of the planner to spend. In the United States old age pension is a part of social security programme, which is a right of every citizen but in India it is a privilege given to very poor, needy, childless, familyless, destitutes and widows. It is not so because we do not have needs but it is because we cannot afford to spend for them. A lot of money is required for social welfare that too of a surplus nature because food and national defence do come before social welfare. The cost of social welfare is rather too much even for the developed countries what to speak of India or other under developed countries. To develop an umbrella for everyone from cradle to grave 'Welfare State' ideology was evolved. As Alan Maynard has remarked "The welfare state was created as a mechanism to mitigate the effects of Beveridge's five giants. Want, disease, ignorance, squalor and idleness". According to the ideal of social justice people must have some basic facilities before they can enter competition where their merit may be judged. As Alan Maynard has said Since the only moral justification for using personal achievement as the basis for distributing rewards is that everyone has equal opportunities for such achievements, the main emphasis is on equality of opportunities and where this cannot be assured, the moral worth of achievement is thereby undermined. Equality is seen as an extension to many, of the freedom actually enjoyed by only the few". In actual practice tax payers are paying for the cost of welfare services but these welfare service are used by non tax payers usually. This situation creates dissatisfaction among tax payers. This is a difficult situation that resources are not according to the need but planning for social welfare activities is an important step to utilise the resources economically and meaningfully.

Social welfare activities not only need resources but also skills of helping. Social work profession tries to inculcate these skills among social workers. An atmosphere where social assistance and, intervention is taking care of the needs gives rise to a welfare state.

REFERENCES

Alan Maynard, Welfare, who pays? Philip Bean ed. *In Defence of Welfare* (London, Tavistock Publication, 1985) p. 142.

Anne Minahan, "Purpose and Objectives of Social Work Revisted" *Social Work,* 26:1 (Jan. 1931) p. 6.

Armando Morales and Bradford, Sheafor *Social Work A Profession of Many Faces,* 5th edition (Boston: Allyn and Bacon, 1989) p. 7.

Belly Baer and Ronald Federico, *Educating The Baccalaureate Social Workers* (Ballinger. Cambridge. 1975) p. 61.

Betty J Piccard, *An Introduction to Social Work* (Illinious: Dorsay Press, 1983) p. 45-46.

H. Kumar, *Social work An Experience and Experiment in India* p. 83.

Harriett Baretleft, "Social Work Practice" *Encyclopedia of Social Work* 16 (New York: National Association of Social Workers, 1970), p. 1479.

Harry Specht, *New Directions for Social Work Practice,* (New Jersey, Printice Hall, , 1938) p. 4.

M.S. Gore, "The Scope of Social Work Practice" Krishan Nair (ed.) *Social Work Education and Social Work Practice in India,* (Madras, Association of School of Social work in India 1981) p. 9.

Morales and Sheafar, *Social Work a Profession of Many Faces* 5th ed. p. 125.

Nitto Neece, *Social Work,* (New Jersey, Printice Hall, 1990), p. 7.

Rex. A, Skidmore and others, *"Introduction to Social Work"* (New Jessey, Printice Hall, 1991) p. 19.

S.H. Pathak, "Social Development and Social Work - Some Unsolved Issues" Nayak and Siddiqui (ed) *Social Work and Social Development* (New Delhi, Gitanjali Publication, 1989) pp. 7-8.

Skidmore and others. *Introduction to Social Work,* p. 13.

Warner. W. Boehm, *Objectives of The Social Work Curriculum in the Future Curriculum Study* 1. (New York, Council on Social Work Education. 1959) p. 54.

Wilensky and Lebeaux, *Industrial Society and Social Welfare,* New York, Free Press 1965), p. 138 quoted by Pothak, Social Welfare, p. 159-160.

3

Social Work Profession: Problems & Issues

Professional social workers assist individuals, groups, or communities to restore or enhance their capacity for social functioning, while creating societal conditions favorable to their goals. The practice of social work requires knowledge of human development and behavior, of social, economic and cultural institutions, and of the interaction of all these factors. In Indian society, social work lacks a precise definition and it is commonly used in terms of charity giving and other types of helping activities for the economically underprivileged and dependent persons. The functioning of most, of the public and private social welfare services reflects the acceptance of such a conception of social work because few of them have even employed any professional social worker and a large majority of them cannot afford to keep one. Moreover, the philosophical and cultural traditions of the society which tend to emphasise the ideals of self-sacrifice and dedication on the one hand and which continue to offer protection and security to the individual within the Indian social structure on the other, reinforce the traditional conception of social work.

Social workers are highly trained and experienced professionals. Only those who have earned social work degrees at the bachelor's, master's or doctoral levels, and completed a minimum number of hours in supervised fieldwork, are "professional social workers."

Professional social workers are found in every facet of community life—in schools, hospitals, mental health clinics, senior centers, elected office, private practices, prisons, military, corporations, and in numerous public and private agencies that serve individuals and families in need. They often specialize in one or more of the following practice areas:

- Community Mental Health
- Employee Assistance
- Private Practice
- Veterans Services
- Child Abuse & Neglect
- Domestic Violence
- Political Development
- Parent Education
- Family Planning
- HIV/AIDS
- School Alternative Programmes
- Difficulties in School
- Gerontology Services
- Community-Based Services
- In-Home Services
- Senile Dementia and Alzheimer's
- Addictions Prevention/Treatment
- Criminal Justice
- Housing Assistance
- Public Welfare
- Employment Services

- Mental Health Therapy
- Disaster Relief
- Military Social Work
- Rural Social Work
- Adoption & Foster Care
- Child Welfare Services
- Family Preservation Services
- Homeless Family Assistance
- Eating Disorders
- Genetics
- Hospital Social Work
- Crisis Intervention
- School Violence
- Hospice and Palliative Care
- Depression
- Institutional Care
- Chronic Pain
- Outpatient Treatment
- Development Disabilities
- International Social Work
- Advocacy, Consulting and Planning

Problems & Issues

This survey shows that the prevailing level of Indian social services and welfare services is extremely low and that most of the voluntary welfare agencies lack the necessary resources to meet some of the basic human needs of common people. Even the Central Social Welfare Board which assists financially more than 12,000 voluntary social welfare agencies has failed to promote the cause of professional social work. Actually, the Board which employs a large number of specialists has not given proper representation to professional social workers. It is true that formal education for social work has taken root and about thirty institutions are offering graduate courses at present, besides many others which are imparting training in related fields both at the graduate and undergraduate levels. It is also true that a number of organisations do exist which continue to promote the cause of professional social work. But there is no denying the fact that both Indian social work education and its professional organisations have been propagating a system of social work which derives its inspiration mainly from American social work philosophy with its ideals, techniques, structure and goals.

As indicated earlier, many of the specialities of Indian social work education such as medical social work, psychiatric social work, family social work, social case work and social group work seem not only irrelevant in the context of the prevailing conditions in Indian society but are also likely to be potentially dysfunctional. The total absence of indigenous study material based upon Indian culture and society has further complicated the applicability of the professional social work as taught in the existing schools of social work. The lack of indigenous base has resulted in a failure to promote firm commitments on the part of both public and private social services in the use of professional social work.

The transmission and diffusion of American social work education with its basic psychological frame of reference have led to an aura of artificiality in the country. Despite the growth of a formal system of training and the establishment of professional organisations, the actual number of persons who have received their professional training does not exceed twenty thousand or so. The occupational structure of the society has not always provided adequate employment opportunities even to this small group of persons. Moreover, many trained social workers are eventually absorbed in positions which bear little relationship to social work raining. As a matter of fact, the professional tradition still seems to exist at a peripheral level, superimposing itself on the traditional conceptions of social work based upon voluntarism, and in many cases the two traditions may stand in direct conflict to each other.

Therefore, the professionals alone have not yet acquired any dominant place to shape and formulate social policies or to administer social welfare organisations. Again, the professional group itself has not developed any social code which the profession also should accept and practice as the fundamental feature of their profession. In view of the dominance of foreign influence on the existing professional social work in India and its lack of integration with the cultural mores of Indian society, there is as yet no agreement on a professional code of ethics for the practice of social work. The profession has failed to develop consciousness of kind and has not created a common platform to express its point of view on broad issues and problems confronting the society. Moreover, the educational institutions offer very few courses on social administration, social planning and social action, and most of the existing courses do not develop intellectual interest and creativity to promote research orientation. In 1975, one of the leading social work educators wrote that social work had remained almost static for more than 25 years. After a decade this still holds true.

As professionalism is ultimately a matter of degree, and professional social work parameters remain elusive, the debate over the boundary between professional and non-professional continues. Nevertheless, scholarly writings have identified relative differences between professional and other kinds of occupational behaviour with respect to certain attributes common to all occupational behaviour. In all societies there is a trend of more and more occupations moving towards professional status, and Indian society is no exception. The rapid growth of urbanisation and industrialisation on the one hand and the adoption of modernisation ideals on the other have been having profound effect upon the occupational structure of the society. Accordingly, the need to develop a more relevant social work education emphasising social administration approach has emerged.

The task of administering social welfare services, private and public, is concerned with the structuring of programmes, services and staff in such a way as to facilitate not only efficient functioning of organisations, but also the collective welfare of people in the society. As the nature and objectives of social welfare organisations are different from other types of organisations, they call for social administration approach. The need for the reorganisation of the existing social welfare organisations on the one hand and for developing new organisations to meet the ever-changing needs of people, especially in a society where directed change has become a socially desirable goal, has to be reflected in the broad-based programmes of social and economic development introduced in the seventh five year plan for the years 1985-90.

Professional Organisations in Social Work

In any profession, professional organisations occupy a unique position, not only for setting standards of educational preparation and certifying professional competence but also for promoting the cause of the profession as well. The Indian Conference of Social Work founded in 1947 has played a significant role in the growth and development of professional social work in India. It is the apex voluntary organisation for individuals and agencies interested in the development and establishment of social welfare organisation to meet the basic needs of the people. It provides a national forum for the discussion of different aspects of social work and meets periodically in different parts of the country. It participates on a consultative level in various committees of the Government of India, state governments and other important national and international agencies. The Conference has branches in almost each state which are generally autonomous in having their own constitution and committees which attempt to represent all kinds of voluntary agencies, centres, schools of social work and individual interests. The Conference also organises national seminars and brings out publications from time to time which are either based on field research undertaken under its own auspices or are based on secondary sources. For a long time the functioning of the Conference has remained dominated by the Tata Institute of Social Sciences and by some prominent women voluntary social workers from the upper classes. The Conference is supported financially by both public and private funds; many state branches have, however, been chronically short of finances with the result that some of them do not employ full-time staff and have no choice but to depend on voluntary workers.

For almost two decades or so, the Conference was a vital force in the field of general social welfare and had played a considerable role in the formulation and preparation of social welfare programmes under the various five year plans. In recent years, its importance has declined partly because of its aging leadership and partly because professional individuals and professional groups seem to have lost their enthusiasm for the promotion of professional social work. It is true that the Indian Conference of Social

Work did promote the cause of professional social work to some extent and established suitable channels of communication with the central and state governmental organisations. But one should also take into consideration the fact that most of the participating members of the Conference, whether organisations or agencies or individuals, generally represent the field of voluntary social work whose basic orientation has been often in conflict with the goals and methods of professional social work. As a result of this conflict, the Conference has not been able to become an effective instrument in the promotion of professional social work.

Moreover, the state branches of the Conference are completely dominated by prominent women from the upper strata who have failed to propogate the cause of professional social work on the one hand and to influence the voluntary social work agencies on the other. Accordingly, it would be fair to say that the Conference does not uphold exclusively the interests of the profession as such. The objectives of the Conference are so broad-based as to include almost any helping activity and any worker from the helping professions. In its relationship with the international organisations the Conference seems to have been highly influenced by American social work philosophy and therefore has maintained very close ties with American social work organisations. As a matter of fact, it is through the Conference and its unique relationship with the Tata Institute of Social Sciences that American social work came to occupy a prominent place not only in Indian social work education but also in the Indian society as a whole. During the years 1961-67, two significant events took place in the history of professional social work, especially in Indian social work education. These are: (1) formation of the Association of Schools of Social Work, and (2) emergence of a national organisation of professional social workers, subsequently re-named the Indian Association of Trained Social Workers. These professional organisations came into existence nearly 25 years after the first school of social work was set up and both of them grew up at almost the same time with the broad objectives of improving the quality of education and propagation of professional social work. In November, 1960 under the leadership of American experts, the Association of Schools of Social Work was established and the representatives of fifteen graduate schools met in Baroda. In addition, representatives from the central government and from the American Technical Cooperation Mission-Social Work Education-India Project also participated in the meeting.

In subsequent years, some steps were taken to develop procedures for accreditation with the result that a set of guidelines was developed to evaluate different schools for the purpose of accreditation. The available evidence, however, shows that there has been little progress during the last 50 years in this direction, and the acceptance of some minimum standards of social work education by the schools themselves still seems to remain a distant goal of the Association. Nevertheless, the Association was successful for more than a decade in promoting, in varying degrees, cooperation among the member schools as well as among many non-member schools. It held annual meetings and seminars where different issues confronting social work education were debated and discussed. During the decade 1970-80, new schools or institutes for the training of social workers were established either as part of one of the existing universities or as autonomous units. The Association has neither been able to prevent their establishment nor has it been successful in influencing them to follow certain basic minimum standards for developing suitable curriculum.

The question of standardisation requires intensive exploration and investigation by the Association not only in cooperation with the central government and state governments but also with different universities.

Unless a uniform system of accreditation on an all India basis is developed and enforced, the development of social work education and programmes on sound lines is likely to proceed very slowly for a long time. In 1965, one committee recommended the establishment of a national social work council, then another committee in 1978 supported this recommendation. But no action seems to have been taken in this behalf so far. The second event related to the emergence of a national organisation of professional social workers in 1961. Earlier there existed an informal organisation of social workers since 1951. This organisation, however, had not been effective in attracting a large number of social workers as members.

The constitution of the Indian Association of Trained Social Workers which was originally adopted in 1961 was modified in 1964, and the Association started publishing a quarterly journal from early 1963. In addition, several chapters of the Association were set up in different parts of the country especially in large cities. The membership of the Association was open to only those who had successfully completed two years graduate training from any school of social work in India and/or abroad, recognised by the Association, and those who paid the membership fee as determined by the General Body of the Association. A provision was made to accept associate members who were students of schools of social work recognised by the Association and paid half the prescribed membership fee, but such members were given no right to vote. The constitution enumerated many objectives as well as methods for their attainment. The Association survived for about

15 years or so and then its importance dwindled with the result that it ceased functioning more than a decade ago. Among the major problems which are believed to be responsible for its decline were those related to the overall lack of identification and commitment by members to the profession of social work especially by those who were employed in business and industrial establishments, personality conflicts among the leadership, non-availability of adequate financial resources and low public image.

The Encyclopedia of Social Work in India lists about 100 national and about 200 regional social welfare organisations. Most of them uphold the cause of voluntary social work but some have been promoting the cause of professional social work in one form or another. Among them, the names of the Association for Moral and Social Hygiene in India, Indian Council for Child Welfare, Indian Adult Education Association, the Family Planning Association of India and the Indian Cooperative Union deserve special mention. These organisations are federated bodies with several branches and affiliates throughout the country and have many trained social workers on their staff. The Association for Moral and Social Hygiene whose primary objective is to eradicate commercialised prostitution and kindred evils has been able to promote the need for social work training programmes for workers in the field of moral rehabilitation; and in 1964 the Association established a Family Life Institute in Delhi, to offer sex education and counselling services. The Indian Council for Child Welfare in cooperation with public welfare organisations has been active in the development of child welfare programmes since 1952 and has organised ad hoc training programmes for child welfare workers from time to time. The Indian Adult Education Association attempts to coordinate the activities of the adult education centres and their workers; it organises periodical seminars, conferences and ad hoc training courses; and it also publishes a quarterly journal to disseminate information relating to adult education programmes. The Family Planning Association of India, though established in 1949, has been playing a prominent role only since 1960 in the promotion of family planning programmes introduced by the Government of India and increasingly trained social workers who have found employment in the family planning centres; and the Association also publishes a quarterly journal of family welfare.

The Indian Cooperative Union founded in 1948 has been interested in the promotion of cooperative movement mainly in cities; it has opened several cooperative stores and established welfare centres selected in slum areas of metropolitan cities. Although these organisations have contributed considerably to the furtherance of social work on a professional basis, they are not professional organisations in social work as they are primarily interested in the promotion of a wide range of programmes and activities of social welfare, and are administered and controlled mainly by social workers who have no formal training in social work. Moreover, they are loosely federated bodies and have neither the legal sanction nor are they in a position to exercise any effective pressure beyond their national office. Even these organisations, at times, subscribe to the traditional conceptions of social work based upon the ideas of self-sacrifice, personal dedication and construction work under the influence of their policy making bodies which do not have commitment to professional social work or to its ethics.

Attributes of a Profession

The professions occupy an important plane in the occupational structure of every society. The history of professions seems to be mainly the history of specialisation, industrialisation and urbanisation. The earliest vocations to move towards professionalisation and to achieve full status of professions were the ministry, law and medicine. The recent trend especially in the industrially advanced societies has been towards the development of more and more vocations into professions. Since the publication of a study by Carr-Saunders and Wilson (1933), a vast amount of literature has become available on the nature and characteristics of the professions. There is, however, no absolute agreement on the definition of a profession. Recently Parsons, a noted American sociologist, has pointed but that the boundaries of the group system we generally call the professions are stilt fluid and indistinct. Students of the professions are increasingly recognising that professionalism is essentially a matter of degree. Many of them have undertaken exhaustive surveys of different professions and have come to specify certain requisites or characteristics which in their opinion differentiate between professional and other forms of occupational behaviour.

Among the most widely accepted characteristics of a profession are included: (a) a system of training through which special competence is acquired and developed; (b) a special body of knowledge, systematic theory and distinct techniques capable of transmission through an orderly and specialised educational system; (c) the existence of the professional organisations for the promotion of standards of service and advancement of interests of their members; (d) a strong sense of loyalty and commitment to the general welfare of society, expressing itself in a code of ethics to govern the behaviour of members, and (e) a wide-spread community recognition to carry out some well-defined functions. It may, however, be noted that different scholars tend to place varying emphasis upon these characteristics. There are some who consider as most essential the requirement of formal technical training accompanied by some institutionalised mode of validating both the adequacy of the training and the competence of trained individuals; there are others who attach the greatest importance to the moral code and recognise that the core criterion is that a profession must have some institutional means of making sure that such competence will be put to socially responsible uses.

Multiplicity of Social Work Conceptions

There is no universally accepted definition of social work even in other societies. Prior to the Tenth International Conference of Social Work, national committees of different countries were asked to prepare, as part of its national report, a statement explaining how the term 'social work' was used. Twenty-four countries submitted their views; even a cursory glance at the definitions reported indicates a complete wilderness and the extreme breadth of the term. As a matter of fact, social work is far from a well-defined field in American society where its practice is relatively established, its methods increasingly standardised and its professional status widely accepted. In its broad sense, the term is generally used to include almost any activity which is intended to help, restore, or promote some aspect of the physical economic, and social well-being of individuals and groups. Mehta's assertion that the role of social services in India is to fight want, disease, squalor, idleness, and ignorance is not unusual. In the same vein many other national leaders have expressed their views on the conception of social work at various meetings of the Indian Conference on Social Work since its establishment in 1947. Even some social work educators, who have been connected with the development of professional social work in the country, have looked at social work somewhat in its broad sense encompassing almost any activity or effort to improve living or working conditions in the community. The official reports published by the Government of India have attempted to clarify the terms 'social service' and 'social welfare' as used in the context of Indian society. The term 'social service' has come to include a broad range of services in such fields as education, health, housing, labour, rehabilitation of refugees, welfare of backward classes, and other social welfare services; it has also been used synonymously with the term 'social policy' to describe what is regarded as a primary responsibility of the state, that is, the provision and maintenance of services for an acceptable standard of social and economic well-being of the entire population.

The term 'social welfare' is, however, limited to that set of services which are intended to meet the special needs of persons and groups who, by reason of a social, economic, physical, or mental handicap are unable to make use of, or are traditionally denied the use of amenities normally provided by the community. Its recipients may be the physically handicapped persons, such as the blind, the deaf, or the crippled; and the socially dependent groups like the orphan, the widow, the destitute, and the mentally retarded; the economically underprivileged groups living in slum areas; and women handicapped by restrictive social traditions. Further the term social welfare has also been used frequently to refer to special services not recognised as a part of the normal social services, such as those of health and education of the youth and children. The provision of settlement of refugees and welfare of backward classes has also been, at times, included under social welfare.

However, the distinction between social service and social welfare is not always maintained. " The object of social welfare", declared in the First Five Year Plan, is the attainment of social health which implies the realisation of such objectives as adequate living standards, the assurance of social Justice, opportunities for cultural development through individual and group self-expressions, and readjustment of human relations leading to social harmony." Similarly, the Second Five Year Plan pointed out that "social welfare is concerned with the entire community, not only of particular sections of the population which may be handicapped in one way or another. Problems which have already come to the fore must no doubt claim attention; equally it is necessary to take steps to prevent the occurrence of new problems".

In the Second and Third Five Year Plans, programmes for the introduction of prohibition as well as programmes of rehabilitation of displaced persons, were included as social welfare; in almost all Plans, programmes of labour welfare, rural welfare and public cooperation were neither formally included under "social services" nor social welfare, but implicitly such programmes were recognised as a part of the total social services and social welfare services which were intended at increasing the social capital of the country. Despite terminological confusion, the Five Year Plans fully recognise that social services and social welfare services are to be organised under governmental and non-governmental auspices directed for the general welfare of people on the one hand and towards the solution of problems at special groups on the other. This, however, does not rule out the existence of social work as individual charity and voluntary service.

Social Work and Professional Organisations

In any profession, professional organisations occupy a unique position, not only for setting standards of educational preparation and certifying professional competence, but for promoting the cause of the profession as well. The Indian Conference of Social Work founded in 1947 has played a significant role in the growth and development of professional social work in India. It is the apex voluntary organisation for individuals and agencies interested in social work and concerned with meeting the social welfare needs of the people. It provides a national forum for the discussion of different aspects of social work and meets periodically (at present every two years) in different parts of the country. The Conference has branches in almost each state, which are generally autonomous in having their own constitution and committees which attempt to represent all kinds of voluntary agencies, centres, schools of social work and individual interests. The Conference also organises national seminars and brings out some publications from time to time which are either based on field researches undertaken in its own auspices or are based on secondary sources. The Conference is supported financially by both public and private funds; many state branches have, however, been chronically short of finances with the result that some of them do not employ full-time staff and have no choice but to depend on voluntary workers.

It is true that the Indian Conference of Social Work has promoted the cause of professional social work and has established suitable channels of communication with central and state governmental organisations. But one should also take into consideration the fact that most of the participating members of the Conference generally represent the field of voluntary social work whose basic orientation has often been in conflict with the goals and methods of professional social work. As a result of this conflict, the Conference has not been able to become an effective instrument in the promotion of professional social work. Moreover, the state branches of the Conference are completely dominated by women from the upper strata of our society who have failed to propagate the cause of professional social work on the one hand and to influence the voluntary social work agencies towards change, in terms of modernisation on a professional basis, on the other. In its relationship with international organisations the Conference seems to be highly influenced by American social work philosophy and, therefore, has maintained very close ties with American social work organisations. As a matter of fact, it is through the Conference and its unique relationship with the Tata Institute of Social Sciences that American social work has come to occupy a prominent place not only in Indian social work education but in the Indian society as a whole.

During the years 1961-67, two significant events took place in the history of professional social work, especially in Indian social work education. These are; (1) formation of the Association of Schools of Social Work, and (2) emergence of a national organisation of professional social workers, subsequently re-named as the Indian Association of Trained Social Workers. It was in November 1960 that the Association of Schools of Social Work came into being. In the subsequent year, some steps were taken to develop procedures for accreditation with the result that a set of guidelines was developed to evaluate different schools for the purpose of accreditation. The available evidence, however, shows that there has been little progress during all these years in this direction and the acceptance of some minimum standards of social work education by the schools themselves still seems to remain a cherished goal of the

Association. Nevertheless, the Association has been able to promote varying degrees of cooperation among the member schools as well as among many non-member schools. The Association has neither been able to prevent the establishment of new schools of social work, nor has it been successful in influencing them to follow certain basic minimum standards for developing suitable curriculum. The question of standardisation requires intensive exploration and investigation by the Association not only in cooperation with the Central government and state governments, but also with different universities. Unless a uniform system of accreditation at an all-India basis is developed and enforced, the establishment of social work training programmes on sound lines and growth of social work as a profession are likely to proceed very slowly for a long time.

The second event related to the emergence of a national organisation of professional social workers in 1961. Earlier, there existed an informal organisation of social workers since 1951, but which had not been effective in attracting a large number of social workers as members. This Association started publishing a quarterly journal from early 1963. In addition, several branches of the Association were set up in different parts of the country, especially in large cities. The membership of the Association is open to only those who have successfully completed two-year post-graduate training from any school of social work in India and/or abroad, recognised by the Association, and those who will pay the membership fee as determined by the General Body of the Association; a provision is also made to accept associate members who are students of schools of social work recognised by the Association and pay one half of the prescribed membership fee, but such members will have no right to vote.

There are several other organisations which have been promoting the cause of professional social work in one form or another. Among them, the names of the Association for Moral and Social Hygiene in India, Indian Council for Child Welfare, Indian Adult Education Association, the Family Planning Association of India, and the Indian Cooperative Union deserve special mention. These organisations are federated bodies with several branches and affiliates throughout the country and have many trained social workers on their staff. Although these organisations have contributed considerably to the furtherance of social work on a professional basis, we cannot call them professional organisations in social work as they are primarily interested in the promotion of a wide range of programmes and activities of social welfare and are administered and controlled mainly by social workers who "have no formal training in social work. In many cases, these organisations tend to subscribe to the traditional conceptions of social work based upon the ideas of self-sacrifice, personal dedication and constructive work under the influence of their policy making bodies which have little commitment to professional social work or its ethics.

Community Commitment and Acceptance of Professional Social Work

Social work is still identified with the philanthropic and social reform movements; it is still considered as a voluntary service to the poor and needy; and it is still practised through organisations, both public and private, which are dominated by the traditional conceptions of social work in terms of charity giving. All the available data show that few social welfare organisations employ trained social workers in rendering direct services to clients; even in supervisory and administrative positions, not many trained social workers are hired. As a matter of fact, there are neither well defined functions of trained social workers nor do we have established positions in different fields of social work practice. Moreover, the professional social worker has not gained acceptance by other well-established professions such as law and medicine to any appreciable extent. It has already been pointed out that except in the case of labour welfare, there are almost no statutory requirements for hiring professional social workers with the result that there exists a lack of consensus regarding the organisations and programmes of service which constitute the field of social work and the person who is entitled to be called a social worker. The concept of general welfare as enunciated in the Constitution of India covers a wide variety of activities of all professional and non-professional workers. It is admitted at all levels of government and even by many voluntary social welfare organisations that some form of training is needed to work in the field of social work, but little differentiation of function has yet emerged to promote the cause of social work as a profession.

The financial position of voluntary social welfare organisations and professional organisations which are expected to promote the cause of the profession constitutes another indicator of the community's commitment and acceptance of professional social work. On the basis of the studies completed by the Central Social Welfare Board and the Indian Conference of Social Work, most of our voluntary welfare agencies do not have sufficient financial resources and, there-more, do not offer employment opportunities to trained social workers. It is also a matter of debate whether the agencies do not have such workers for want of adequate funds or they have not yet been convinced in the superior performance and competence of the professional social worker. The available evidence points out that most of them have not given due recognition to professional social work itself. The financial status of professional organisations themselves is far from being satisfactory. It is reported that the Indian Association of the Alumni of Schools of Social Work which is known now as the Indian Association of Trained Social Workers received a grant of one thousand rupees for the preparation of a directory of trained social workers from the American Women's Club of Delhi; and the Indian Conference of Social Work undertook the study of the employment position and functions of professional social workers in India through a grant from the United States Department of Health, Education, and Welfare.

For many other professional activities, both schools of social work and professional organisations of social workers have often received funds from foreign sources, mainly from public and private agencies in the United States. The early attempts to bring Indian schools of social work together in order to develop uniform standards of training and to forge joint plans for the promotion of professional social work were also initiated and financed by the United States through the Office of Technical Cooperation Mission in Delhi.

Need For Indigenous Base

The above survey of the field of social work shows that the prevailing level of Indian social services and welfare services is extremely low and that most of the voluntary welfare agencies lack the necessary resources to meet some of the basic human needs of food, shelter, health education, and employment. It is true that formal education for social work has taken root in the country and about thirty institutions are offering graduate courses at present; besides, many others are imparting training at the undergraduate level. It is also true that several organisations exist which continue to promote the cause of professional social work. But there is no denying the fact that both Indian social work education and its professional organisations have been propagating a system of social work which derives its inspiration mainly from American social work philosophy with its ideals, techniques, structure, and goals. As indicated earlier, many of the specialties of Indian social work education such as medical social work, psychiatric social work, family social work, social case work and social group work seem not only irrelevant in the context of the prevailing conditions in Indian society, but also are likely to be potentially dysfunctional.

The total absence of indigenous study material based upon Indian culture and society has further complicated the applicability of the professional social work as taught in the existing schools of social work. The lack of indigenous base has also failed to promote firm commitments on the part of both public and private social services in the use of professional social work. The transmission and diffusion of American social work education with its basic psychological frame of reference have led to an aura of artificiality in the country. Despite the growth of a formal system of training and establishment of professional organisations, the actual number of persons who have received their professional training does not exceed a few thousand so far. The occupational structure of the society has not always provided adequate employment opportunities even to this small group of persons. Moreover, many trained social workers are eventually absorbed in such positions which bear little relationship to social work training. As a matter of fact, the professional tradition still seems to exist at a peripheral level, superimposing itself on the traditional conceptions of social work based upon voluntarism, and in many cases the two traditions may stand in direct conflict with each other. Therefore, the professionals alone have not yet acquired any dominant right to practise social work. Again, the professional group does not have a moral code which has come to be recognised as the most important feature of any profession. In view of the dominance of foreign influence on the existing professional social work in India and its lack of integration with the cultural mores of Indian society, there is as yet no agreement on a professional code of ethics for the practice of social work. Admitted that professionalism is ultimately a matter of degree and among the scholars as well as the public, the debate over the boundary between professional and non-professional continues.

Nevertheless, scholarly writings have identified relative differences between professional and other kinds of occupational behaviour with respect to certain attributes common to all occupational behaviour. In all societies there is a movement of more and more occupations towards professional status and Indian society is no exception. The rapid growth of urbanisation and industrialisation on the one hand and the adoption of modernisation ideals on the other are having profound effects upon the occupational structure of Indian society. Accordingly, the need to develop social administration approach to social work has emerged. The task of administering social welfare services is concerned with the structuring of programmes, services and staff in such a way as to facilitate not only efficient functioning of organisations, but also the collective welfare of people in the society. As the nature and objectives of social welfare organisations are different from other types of organisations, they call for a social administration approach. The demand for the organisation and development of new social welfare services to meet the ever-changing needs of the people, especially in a society where directed change has become a socially desirable goal, has to be taken into consideration in social administration.

Moreover, in a society where a large majority of people has little tradition of participation in the formulation of social welfare programmes, the professional social worker has a special responsibility to promote civic awareness about social problems and to enlist cooperation from different sections of population for solving them or for minimising their incidence. Social research will also become an integral part of social administration, not only to collect some of the basic social and economic data, bat also to study the effectiveness of services.

Social Work: Specialisations and Indigenous Study Material

An analysis of the bulletins of the schools of social work indicates that they offer training in such specialised fields of study as labour welfare, tribal welfare, rural welfare, medical social work, family social work, psychiatric social work, institutional and correctional administration and community organisation. The growth of many of these areas has been largely influenced by the American pattern of social work education, having little regard to the prevailing social, cultural, economic and political 'conditions in Indian society. It is an accepted fact that at the present time there are no well-defined categories of welfare personnel for which social work training is considered essential except in the case of labour welfare.

Actually, it is well known that in the field of mental health our level of services is extremely poor and provision for the treatment of persons suffering from mental disorders and mental deficiency is not only inadequate, but there are scarcely enough institutions and workers to provide barely elementary forms of custodial care. In this context, the need to create a class of functionaries, called psychiatric social workers who will study the patient as a person in his social situation and analyse environmental factors hardly seems to be justified. Moreover, the therapeutic value of Hindu religion which incorporates several systems of yoga practices to promote emotional balance, physical poise, and peace of mind, and the existence of indigenous medicines to relieve both physical and mental illnesses are two unique forces which are reported to have minimised the incidence of mental morbidity and continue to have a wider acceptance especially among the rural population.

Social work education, however, does not take them into consideration at all. Family social work, another specialisation which is offered by many schools, is often combined with child welfare. The main objective of family social work is considered to help the individual and members of his family in attaining harmonious relationships in their family life so as to prevent individual and family disorganisation. This is achieved through the use of social casework which includes marriage counselling, family life education, and financial assistance.

Perhaps, the joint family system has changed considerably both in its structure and function as a result of increasing urbanisation, industrialisation, and modernisation during the last three decades. But even today, the joint family continues to provide all the services to its members in times of need. Problems of marital conflict, disturbed parent-child relationships, fatherless families, unmarried mothers, single adults who are separated from their families and the aged do exist in India, though scanty data is available about these problems and no reliable statistics exist.

At the same time, we do know that the magnitude of

these problems is not so great because they have neither weakened the existing structure and functioning of our society, nor have they got any recognition in the Indian Five Year Plans which are aimed at achieving social and economic development of the country on a panned basis in the years ahead. Moreover, the existence of family welfare agencies in the sense in which family social work is interpreted in the United States is still unknown in the country. For a long time, professional social work has been highly correlated with the field of labour welfare not only by some of the schools themselves, but also by the employers, government officials and leaders of voluntary social work.

The emergence of the fields of personnel management and business administration on the one hand and the development of social insurance, growth of trade unionism and social security measures and increasing acceptance of welfare activities by the employer on the other, have confronted the schools of social work with a fundamental dilemma as to whether new roles of industrial relations and personnel management belong to the field of social work. From the description of functions, as presented by social work educators, which the welfare officers are usually called upon to perform today, it seems doubtful if these functions belong to the field of professional social work. In the past decade, there has been an increasing trend toward the establishment of new centres or institutes for specialised training in labour welfare outside social work which offer not only courses on labour welfare, but also in industrial relations and personnel management as well.

Recently, the Tata Institute instituted a separate degree programme for personnel management and labour welfare apart from the social work degree, but within its existing framework. The other schools are still hesitant to change the established pattern or to abolish this field of specialisation from their training programme, because this specialisation is the only one for which social work training is statutorily recognised, for which major demand exists among the applicants seeking admission to the schools of social work and for which relatively more employment opportunities are available and with better salaries. It may also be pointed out here that labour welfare specialisation happens to be the field of study for which the schools are generally ill-equipped in terms of training, because most of the faculty members usually do not have the requisite experience of working in industrial settings, the field work consists mainly of observation and courses of instructions are not necessarily consistent with the philosophy of social work. The other specialisations offered by many schools of social work relate to the fields of rural welfare, tribal welfare, and urban community development, and at least in one school, specialisation is provided in social research as well. Almost 80% of the Indian population still lives in rural areas where levels of living are very poor and that large-scale programmes of rural development have been introduced throughout the country.

Although the schools of social work have been offering courses on rural welfare from the very beginning and some schools claim to have specialisation, it is a well-known fact that Indian professional social work has failed to establish its role in the field of rural welfare. The very fact that a large number of centres, institutes, and orientation camps are functioning for the training of different categories of rural welfare personnel outside the professional social work indicates the failure of the schools to assume responsibility for the training of such personnel.

Tribal welfare is considered a major field of specialisation by a few schools, though the Tata Institute used to be the only school for several years, where adequate training facilities had existed and even here this specialisation has declined. In all the Five Year Plans, the welfare of backward classes including tribal welfare has been given special attention. This is understandable in view of the fact that almost one hundred million persons are classified as belonging to backward classes in the country. The Study completed by the Indian Conference on Social Work has, however, revealed that the number of social workers working in the field of tribal welfare is very insignificant. Two major reasons why social workers do not take up positions in this field seem to relate to the fact that the tribal welfare settings are generally inaccessible and provide inadequate monetary rewards; secondly, a number of Tribal Research Institutes exist outside the field of social work which offer training facilities fop tribal welfare worker, and these Institutes are located in such places where comprehensive programmes for tribal welfare have been established.

In addition, Indian anthropologists have also been interested both in the study of tribal life and in the provision of welfare activities as reflected through the existence of a special Department of Anthropology and Office of the Commissioner for the Scheduled Castes and Tribes in the Central government. Indeed, in the fields of both rural welfare and tribal welfare, the problems of social administration, community organisation and development, directed change, and social research seem to be the most important areas for which social welfare personnel is needed. Many schools of social work offer a specialisation designated as institutional and correctional administration. The care of the destitute, the handicapped, the delinquent, and the criminal is mainly provided through institutions, both public and private.

The ultimate goal of the institutional care is said to be the prevention of the incidence of social problems and rehabilitation of persons who become inmates of the institutions. But if the existing level of social services is any indication, it is fair to say that even our institutional services are far from being satisfactory and are constantly experiencing chronic shortages of adequate space, decent housing, proper equipment and qualified staff. Specifically in the field of correctional administration, the impact of professional social work seems to be insignificant. The level of services in terms of probation and parole, separation of the juveniles from the adult criminal, provision of vocational training and after-care and training of personnel for correctional administration is extremely low even today. The basic orientation of this training programme seems to be conditioned by American social case-work approach with little emphasis upon the practice of social administration. It may be noted here that in the United States itself the professional social work has not made considerable progress in the field of correctional administration despite the fact that the level of services is fairly well-developed at least in the institutions which function directly under the auspices of the federal government.

Again, at the present time, one-fourth of the Indian population lives in urban areas, and cities having 10,000 and more inhabitants have been on the increase in the last two decades. The need for specialised programmes of urban redevelopment and urban community development has been accepted in the Fourth Five Year Plan; social welfare programmes are also being intensified at least in large cities; family planning programmes are being introduced on a wider scale than ever before; and slum clearance and improvement programmes have been initiated to improve the living conditions in Indian cities. It is true that all schools of social work are offering courses on urban community development and organisation; but the Tata Institute is the only school which has a well-established specialisation in this field.

The working of the Delhi Pilot Project, established by the Delhi Municipal Corporation in 1959 to promote the growth of community life and to encourage the development of citizen participation in the programmes of social welfare has demonstrated that we need several categories of welfare personnel in the field of urban community development. Moreover, the professional social workers have not yet established their specialised roles in this field on the basis of their competence. In the context of Indian society, as their fields of health, education, and social welfare co-exist and often interpenetrate at a local level, community development both in the urban and rural areas is essentially a multi-dimensional activity. Accordingly, any specialisation offered in community organisation needs to be established on an inter-disciplinary basis and which should take into consideration all the basic social sciences. The existing courses of training in community organisation at the schools of social work rely heavily on American social work and tend to neglect contributions from the fields of economics, political science, sociology, and cultural anthropology.

Moreover, it may be noted that academic courses concerning social group work and field work practice in recreational centres which have come from American social work and are widely accepted as a part of the existing social work curriculum require considerable re-organisation if they have to serve essential societal functions. Scholars who have studied and analysed the growth of professions agree that one of the fundamental characteristics of any profession is the availability of a body of systematic knowledge in such forms as tested knowledge, hypothetical knowledge which requires transformation into tested knowledge and assumptive knowledge or "practice wisdom" that requires transformation into hypothetical and hence tested knowledge. The development of different forms of knowledge, we are further told by those who have undertaken studies in the field of sociology of knowledge, is not only conditioned by the social, economic and cultural patterns of life but also by the political forces at a given historical moment. It is well known that societies, which have been under the foreign political rule for varying lengths of time, developed their higher educational system on the lines of the Western education, and consequently the growth of indigenous knowledge has been rather slow and in many branches of study it has been conspicuous by its absence. Ironically, sociologists of knowledge seem to have neglected this area of study with reference to such societies. In the wake of of enthusiasm that marked the attainment of independence for India in 1947, there has been a new awareness of the broader scope of the responsibilities our universities most have. The report of the University Education Commission, appointed in November 1948, was the first comprehensive attempt at the re-organisation of our higher education. The report emphatically stated that the universities as the makers of the future could not persist in the old patterns and that they have to change their objectives and methods if they are to function effectively in the national life.

We have seen another monumental, report of the Education Commission (1966) which has pointed out that the most important and urgent reform needed in education is to transform it in such a way as to relate it to the life, needs and aspirations of the people and thereby make it a powerful instrument of social, economic, and cultural transformation necessary for the realisation of national goals. This transformation, it is agreed at all hands, requires the development of an indigenous intellectual tradition on the one hand and accumulation of indigenous knowledge on the other. But social work education and study material present a unique case where the influence of foreign elements is almost universal and there is a crying need for the development of indigenous scholarship.

Although the first professional school of social work was established more than thirty years ago, there does not exist a single textbook on Indian social work taking into consideration Indian social, economic and political conditions on the one hand, and the contributions of Indian social scientists on the other. A cursory glance at the books recommended, suggested or required for the various courses as mentioned in the bulletins indicate that the schools tend to make an excessive use of foreign material written by Western scholars, especially Americans, for most of the courses of study.

As a matter of fact, the available publications written by Indian professional social workers on different aspects of Indian society also seem to be based mainly on Western concepts, theories, and knowledge, and they have often failed to incorporate the contributions of Indian social scientists. Few schools have even suggested reports of Indian governmental committees, boards, and commissions which ape sources of primary data about our cultural, social, economic, and political conditions of the country. It seems that Indian schools, unlike those in the United States, have found a body of formulated concepts and theories and techniques of social work from American social work literature on which they could draw upon for the planning of their educational programmes. These concepts, theories and techniques nurtured and nourished in a different culture have been transplanted to Indian schools without much modification. The books that are used for classroom teaching expounding the philosophy and principles of social work have mostly been written in the United States with the American audience in mind.

Although American study material is increasingly being resented, there is a general acceptance of the American social work philosophy and principles at all the schools, and hence there exists a wide gap between the theoretical knowledge of the student and the reality situations to which he is constantly exposed through field work experience.

SOCIAL WORK AS PROFESSION: MAIN PROBLEMS

The professions occupy an important place in the occupational structure of every society. The history of the professions seems to be mainly history of specialisation, industrialisation and urbanisation. The earliest vocations to move towards professionalisation and to achieve full status of professions were the ministry, law and medicine. The recent trend especially in the industrially advanced societies has been towards the development of more and more vocations into professions. Since the publication of a study by Carr-Saunders and Wilson (1933), a vast amount of literature has become available on the nature and characteristics of the professions. There is, however, no absolute agreement on the definition of a profession.

Almost two decades ago, Parsons, a noted American sociologist, pointed out that the boundaries of the group system we generally call the professions are still fluid and indistinct. The same picture continues to prevail even today. Students of the professions are increasingly recognising the fact that professionalism is essentially a matter of degree. Many of them have undertaken exhaustive surveys of different professions and have come to specify certain characteristics which in their opinion differentiate professional from other forms of occupational behaviour.

Among the most widely accepted characteristics of a profession are: (1) a system of education and training through which special competence is acquired and developed; (b) a special body of knowledge, systematic theory and distinct techniques capable of transmission through an orderly and specialised educational system; (c) the existence of professional organisations for the promotion of standards of service and advancement of interests of their members; (d) a strong sense of loyalty and commitment to the general welfare of society, expressing itself in a code of ethics to govern the behaviour of members, and (3) a widespread community recognition to carry out some well-defined functions. It may, however, be noted that different scholars tend to place varying emphasis upon these characteristics.

There are some who consider as most essential the requirement of formal technical training accompanied by some institutionalised mode of validating both the adequacy of the training and the competence of trained individuals; there are others who attach the greatest importance to the moral code, and recognise that the core criterion is that a profession must have some institutional means of making sure that such competence will be put to socially responsible uses.

Conceptions of Multiple Social Work

Social work as a profession is still in its infancy in India. The very term social work lacks a precise definition. As a matter of fact, social work is far from a well-defined field even in American society where its practice is relatively established, its methods increasingly standardised and its professional status widely accepted. In India, the term is generally used to include almost any activity which is intended to help, restore, or promote some aspect of the physical, economic, and social well-being of individuals and groups. In its restricted sense it has come to refer to charity-giving and other types of helping activities for the economically under-privileged and dependent persons. The functioning of most of the public and private social welfare services reflects the acceptance of such a conception of social work because not many of them employ any professional social worker, and a large majority of them cannot afford to keep even one worker.

Moreover, the basic philosophical and cultural traditions of the Indian society continue to emphasise the ideals of self-sacrifice and dedication, which in turn offer protection and security to the individual within the Indian social structure. In recent times, as is well known, Gandhiji also revived the old tradition of social service, and influenced not only the establishment of services for the weaker sections of the population but also promoted the training of workers on the ideals of dedication and self-sacrifice. The official reports published by the Government of India have attempted to clarify the terms social service and social welfare as used in the context of Indian society.

The term social service has come to include a broad range of services in such fields as education, health, housing, labour, rehabilitation of refugees, welfare of backward classes, and other social welfare services; it has also been used synonymously with the term social policy to describe what is regarded as a primary responsibility of the state which emphasises the provision and maintenance of services for an acceptable standard of social and economic well-being of the entire population.

The term social welfare is, however, limited to that set

of services which are intended to meet the special needs of persons and groups who by reason of social, economic, physical, or mental handicaps are unable to make use of, or are traditionally denied the use of amenities normally provided by the community. Its recipients may be the physically handicapped persons, such as the blind, the deaf or the crippled; and the socially dependent groups like the orphans, the widows, the destitutes, and the mentally retarded, or the economically under-privileged groups living in slum areas, and women handicapped by restrictive social traditions. Further provision of special services of health and education for children and youth, the settlement of refugees, and welfare of backward classes has also been, at times, included under social welfare.

Absence of Systematic Knowledge

Although the first professional school of social work was established more than fifty years ago, there is not a single basic textbook on Indian social welfare taking into consideration indigenous elements of social, economic and political life. Few schools even suggest reports of Indian governmental committees, boards, and commissions which are sources of primary data about contemporary cultural, social, economic, and political conditions of the country. As a matter of fact, the available publications written by Indian professional social workers on different aspects of Indian society also seem to be based mainly on Western concepts, theories and knowledge, and they have often failed to incorporate the contributions of Indian social scientists. Indian social work education has found a ready-made body of formulated concepts, principles, theories and techniques from American social work literature. The study material used in all institutions is not only exclusively American but also most of it was published in the sixties and even in the fifties.

Scholars who have studied and analysed the growth of professions agree that one of the fundamental characteristics of any profession is the availability of a body of systematic knowledge in such forms as tested knowledge, hypothetical knowledge which requires transformation into tested knowledge and assumptive knowledge or practice wisdom that requires transformation into hypothetical and hence tested knowledge. The development of different forms of knowledge is not only conditioned by the social, economic and cultural patterns of life but also by the political forces at a given historical moment. It is well known that societies which have been under the foreign political rule for varying lengths of time developed their higher educational system on the lines of the western education, and consequently the growth of indigenous knowledge has been rather slow and in many branches of study it has been conspicuous by its absence. Ironically, sociologists of knowledge seem to have neglected this area of study with reference to such societies.

In the wake of enthusiasm that marked the attainment of independence for India in 1947, there has been a new awareness of the broader scope of the responsibilities which universities must have. The report of the University Education Commission appointed in November, 1948, was the first comprehensive attempt at the reorganisation of our higher education. The report emphatically stated that the universities as the makers of the future could not persist in the old patterns and that they had to change their objectives and methods if they were to function effectively in national life.

In 1966, another monumental report of the Education Commission pointed out that the most important and urgent reform needed in education is to transform it in such a way as to relate it to the life, needs and aspirations of the people, and thereby make it a powerful instrument of social, economic and cultural transformation necessary for the realisation of national goals. This transformation, it is agreed at all hands, requires the development of an indigenous intellectual tradition on the one hand and accumulation of indigenous knowledge on the other. But social work education and study material present a unique case where the influence of foreign elements is almost universal and there is a crying need for the development of indigenous scholarship.

In 1985, there was yet another report which once again brought out the fact that educational institutions as entities were generally oblivious of and unconcerned with the problems, potentials and characteristics of their environment. This has resulted in lack of orientation and dysfunctionality of research and educational content, lack of support from the environment and the isolation of the teachers and students from the reality of life and the world of work.

On the other hand, the community around these institutions is also a great loser since it is denied the opportunity of enriching itself and finding solutions to its problems through the intervention and support of a technically knowledgeable and mentally and physically agile group of people. This description applies with greater force to social work education than to any other field of education because the present system continues to lack social relevance even today.

Community Commitment and Acceptance of Professional Social Work

Social work is still identified with the philanthropic and social reform movements; it is still considered a voluntary service to the poor and the needy; and it is still practised through organisations, public and private, which are dominated by the traditional conceptions of social work in terms of charity giving. All the available data show that only a few social welfare organisations employ trained social workers in rendering direct services to clients; and even in supervisory and administrative positions, not many trained social workers are employed. At the present time there are neither well-defined functions of trained social workers nor do we have established positions for different fields of social work practice.

It has already been pointed out that except in the case of labour welfare, there are almost no statutory requirements for hiring professional social workers with the result that there exists lack of consensus on what organisations and programmes of service constitute the field of social work and who is entitled to be called a social worker. The concept of general welfare as enunciated in the constitution of India covers a wide variety of activities of all professional and non-professional workers. It is admitted at all levels of government and even by many voluntary social welfare organisations that some form of training is needed to work in the field of social work but little differentiation of function has yet emerged between the professionals and non-professionals to promote the cause of social work as a profession.

The other professions such as law and medicine have shown little acceptance of social work as a profession. Although schools of social work have been offering the specialisation of medical and psychiatric social work for more than three decades, neither health nor medical settings have given widespread recognition, and their total number is still insignificant and is limited only to the metropolitan cities of Bombay, Delhi and Madras. As a matter of fact, social workers are employed in many settings which are mainly engaged in educational, administrative and research activities rather than in offering direct service to clients. In view of the fact that there are no requirements of registration or any form of licensing, the distinction between professional and non-professional is not maintained in society in general and by other professions in particular while considering the place of social work and social worker. Moreover, there are few positions which require training in professional social work as essential; even the very existence of positions known as social work positions is at its minimum in the total occupational structure of Indian society. Actually, the training programmes in social work themselves are often confronted with the problem of gaining acceptance by other disciplines in the university system. Most universities have not introduced social work as a field of study as yet and there are others where departments or schools of social work do exist but the universities have not been able to recognise the value of field work training, and in most cases such departments have been placed under the faculties of social sciences, without recognising the professional status of the social work discipline itself or its training programmes.

The financial position of voluntary social welfare organisations and professional organisations which are expected to promote the cause of the profession constitutes another indicator of the community's commitment and acceptance of professional social work. It has already been pointed out on the basis of the studies completed by the Central Social Welfare Board and the Indian Conference of Social Work that most of our voluntary welfare agencies do not have sufficient financial resources and therefore do not offer employment opportunities to trained social workers. It is also a matter of debate whether the agencies do not have such workers for want of adequate funds or they have not yet been convinced of the superior performance and competence of the professional social worker. The available evidence points out that most of them have not given due recognition to professional social work itself.

The Indian Association of Trained Social Workers once received a grant of about one hundred US dollars for the preparation of a directory of trained social workers from the American Women's Club of Delhi; and the Indian Conference of Social Work undertook the study of the employment position and functions of professional social workers in India through a grant from the United States Department of Health, Education and Welfare. Recently, proceedings of one of the seminars organised by the Association of the Schools were also published with a foreign grant. For many other professional activities both schools of social work and professional organisations of social workers have often received funds from foreign sources, mainly from public and private agencies in the United States. The early attempts to bring Indian schools of social work together in order to develop uniform standards of training and to forge joint plans for the promotion of professional social work were also initiated and financed by the United States through the office of Technical Cooperation Mission located in Delhi.

Commitment to Public Welfare and Social Ethics

Any survey of social work literature as well as of the objectives of social work organisations does indicate that the profession is committed to the promotion of general public welfare. However, this commitment exists in the context of the broad-based goals of Indian society as enuniciated in the constitution of India. It is through a series of five year plans that systematic and comprehensive programmes have been launched to promote the constitutional goals of public welfare and to bring about directed changes in the society. There is an ever-increasing realisation that social welfare activities should be strengthened and intensified if any programme of social and economic development has to become effective. Along with public welfare services, the tradition of voluntary social welfare continues to exist, and more than ten thousand voluntary organisations are functioning. But most of the voluntary organisations are run on traditional lines and they do not generally employ trained social workers partly due to lack of adequate financial resources and partly because of non-acceptance of professional social work. Moreover, the professionals themselves have not proved their superior competence as yet. There is also a great deal of duplication and overlapping in the field of voluntary social welfare with the result that there is no functional coordination of services at local level. Communal, religious and parochial considerations have also created vested interests which often hamper their reorganisation and modernisation, and consequently most of the voluntary organisations have not played any significant role in the growth and development of social work as a profession.

As stated earlier, the tradition of Gandhian constructive work is deeply roorted and continues to influence social work in one form or another. As a matter of fact, social work is still interpreted in this tradition and is regarded as a voluntary service, actuated by a strong sense of altruism. The political struggle initiated under Gandhiji was not only concerned with the attainment of political freedom from the British government, but has also included programmes of social and economic development especially for the low castes and low income groups.

Most social work organisations are, therefore, highly influenced by the Gandhian social work philosophy based on constructive work and voluntary service. Several centres or institutions also exist for the training of constructive workers in different parts of the country. For a long time, no systematic attempt has been made to establish cooperation between professional social work and Gandhian social work. Broadly speaking, both traditions function side by side even today but they have not come to any mutual understanding so as to launch cooperative projects. Neither the professional schools nor the professional workers have made any attempt to incorporate indigenous elements in the curricula of the training programmes. Students of professions agree that professionals must follow an identifiable set of values, and display attitudes based upon these values, and which should provide the administration of social welfare services and his relationship with the outside world. These values and attitudes are frequently incorporated as a part in codes of ethics and enumerate the services to clients, the rights of clients, and the obligations and rights of workers themselves.

REFERENCES

Chatterjee, B., "Urban Community Development in India: The Delhi Pilot Project", in Roy Turner, *Indian's Urban Suture* (Berke-ley, 1962).

Das, S., Gupta (ed.). *Towards a Philosophy of Social Work in India* (New Delhi, Popular Books, 1967).

Edward Blunt (ed.) *Social Service is India* (London, 1938); Charles Heimsath, *Indian Nationalism and Hindu Social Reform* (Princeton, 1964); K. P. Karunakaran, *Religious and Political Awakening in India* (Delhi, 1965); and S. Natarajan, *A Century of Social Reform in India* (Bombay, 1965).

Edward Shils, *The Intellectual Between Tradition and Modernity: The Indian Situation* (The Hague, 1961).

Ernest Greenwood, "Attributes of a Profession", *Social Work,* (U.S.A.), July, 1957, pp. 45-55; Also see, his modified version "Attributes of a Profession", in S.K. Lal and others (ed.) *Readings in the Sociology of Professions,* Delhi, Gian (1988).

Gangrade, K.D., "Conflicting Value System and Social Casework", *Indian Journal of Social Work,* January 1964.

Gokhale, S.D. , *Social Welfare, Legend and Legacy* (Bombay, Popular Prakashan, 1975).

Gore, M.S., "Cultural Perspectives In Social Work In India"; *International Social Work,* July 1966.

Gore, M.S., Social *Work and Social Work Education* (Bombay, 1965).

Government of India, *Report of the University Education Commission* (New Delhi, 1950).

Government of India, see. *Report of the Education Commission in India* (New Delhi, 1966); and Edward Shils, *The Intellectual Between Tradition and Modernity: The Indian Situation* (The Hague, 1961).

Hans Nagpaul, " Community Development for Urban Areas in India", *International Review of Community Development,* No. 9, 1962.

Hans Nagpaul, "Analysis of Social Work Study Material in India", *Indian Journal of Social Research,* No. 3, 1970.

Hans Nagpaul, "Appraisal of Social Work Specialties", *Indian Journal of Social Work,* July 1970.

Hans Nagpaul, "Dilemmas of Social Work Education in India", *Indian Journal of Social Work,* October, 1967.

Hans Nagpaul, "Education for Social Work in India", in S. K. Kinduka (ed.) *Social Work in India* (Allahabad, Kitab Mahal, 1965), pp. 241-268; *Indian Journal of Social Work,* April 1967, Special Issue; and *Report of the Review Committee on Social Work Education in Indian Universities* (New Delhi, 1965).

Jivraj Mehta, "Presidential Address", *Indian Journal of Social Work,* June 1950, p. 23.

Lee Taylor, *Occupational Sociology* (New York, 1988); and Harold Wilensky and Charles Lebeaux, *Industrial Society and Social Welfare* (New York, 1938); also see the special issue on "Profes-sions", *Daedalus* (U.S.A.), Fall, 1963.

Lee Taylor, *Occupational Sociology* (New York, Oxford, 1968); Richard Hall, *Occupations and the Social Structure* (Englewood Cliffs, N.J., Prentice Hall, 1969); and Eliot Freidson (ed.). *The Professions and Their Prospects* (Beverly Hills, Ca. Sage. 1973).

Majumdar, R.C. (ed.). *The History and Culture of the Indian People* (Bombay, Vidya Bhawan, 1954). For a brief review see, Hans Nagpual, "Religio-Philosophical Foundations", and "Persistence of Traditional Elements", in his *Culture, Education and Social Welfare* (New Delhi, S. Chand, 1980).

Marshall Clinard, *Slums and Community Development* (New York, 1966).

Mujamdar, A.M., *Social Welfare in India, Mahatma Gandhi's Contributions* (New Delhi, Asia, 1965).

Mukundarao, K., "Social Work in India: Indigenous Culture Bases and the Processes of Modernisation", *International Social Work,* No. 3, 1969.

Muzumdar, A.M., *Social Welfare in India, Mahatma Gandhi's Contributions* (New Delhi, 1965).

Phadke, S., "Values of Social Work and Cultural Impediments in Their Acceptance and Practice", *Social Work Forum,* July 1966.

Ranade, S.N., "Social Work Education in India", in *Social Welfare, Legend and Legacy, Ibid;* pp. 198-200.

Talcott Parsons, "Professions", in *International Encyclopedia of the Social Sciences* (New York, 1968), Vol. pp. 536-547.

Talcott Parsons, "Professions", in *International Encyclopedia of the Social Sciences,* (New York, Macmillan, 1968), pp. 536-547; also see, the special issue on Professions; *Deadalus* (U.S.A.), Fall, 1963.

Wadia, A.R., "Ethical and Spiritual Values in the Practice of Social Work", in A. R. Wadia (ed.) *History and Philoso-phy of Social Work in India* (Bombay, 1961), p. 3.

Werner W. Boehm, *Objectives of the Social Work Curriculum of the Future* (New York, 1959), p. 41.

4

Career in Social Work

BACHELOR'S DEGREE

A bachelor's degree is usually an undergraduate academic degree awarded for a course or major that generally lasts for three, four, or in some cases and countries, five or six years. It may also be the name of a postgraduate degree, such as a Bachelor of Civil Law, the Bachelor of Music, or the Bachelor of Philosophy.

Honors Degrees and Academic Distinctions

Under the new British system, and those influenced by it, such as the American, Canadian, Irish, Jordanian, Indian, Malaysian, Maltese, Sri Lankan, Singaporean, Hong Kong and Australian systems, undergraduate degrees are differentiated either as *pass degrees* or as *honours degrees*, the latter sometimes denoted by the appearance of "(Hons)" after the degree abbreviation. An honours degree generally requires a higher academic standard than a pass degree, and in Maltese, Singaporean, Australian, New Zealand, Scottish, Sri Lankan, Malaysian and some Canadian universities an extra year of study. Previously in the UK Polytechnics, an honours degree took one more year of study than an ordinary degree. This applies in Scotland with ordinary MA and MA(Hons) degrees (which are the equivalent of English first (BA) degrees). In England now, most first degrees are assumed to be honours as Third Class honours are actually a relatively low standard. In Scotland there also exist *Designated Degrees*. But other universities, such as MIT, do not make any such distinctions.

Southern Africa

In the Namibian, South African and Zimbabwean systems, an honours degree must include a project course that the students must complete individually, with different projects carried out by each student.

Canada

Depending on the province, a bachelor's degree takes either three or four years to complete. Traditionally, a three-year degree is also called a *pass degree* or *general degree*, and a four-year degree is also called an *honours degree*. In provinces that grant three-year bachelor's degrees, a student may choose to complete an additional year of studies to obtain a four-year honours degree.

Some Canadian universities no longer offer three-year pass degrees, and have started to grant four-year honours degrees exclusively. In general, obtaining a bachelor's honours degree requires completion of a number of full year credits, completion of one or more majors or a specialist program, and maintaining a grade point average above a certain minimum.

An honours bachelor's degree is generally a prerequisite for admission into graduate studies in Canada.

England, Wales and Northern Ireland

The degrees awarded carry a designation related to the broad subject area such as BA, BSc, BEng etc. The majority of Bachelor's degrees are now honours degrees.

Prior to the mid 20th century some candidates (but not, for example, at Oxford or Cambridge) would take an Ordinary degree, and then be selected to go on for a final year for the Honours degree. A first degree course is usually three years, but it might be reduced to two either by direct second year entry (for people who have done foundation degrees or changed subject or similar) or by doing compressed courses (which are being piloted by several newer universities).

For funding reasons (funding for undergraduate programmes is automatic, funding for postgraduate programmes is not) it is becoming increasingly common to skip the Bachelor's stage entirely and go straight to Masters level on a four year (five year if with industrial experience) course (which often shares the first two years with the equivalent Bachelor's course).

Honours degrees are of a superior academic standard. An Honours degree is always awarded in one of four classes depending upon the marks gained in the final assessments and examinations. The top students are awarded a first class degree, the next best, an upper second class degree (usually referred to as a 2:1), the next a lower second class degree (usually referred to as a 2:2), and those with the lowest marks gain a third class degree. An *Ordinary* or *unclassified* degree (which does not give the graduate the right to add *(Hons)*) may be awarded if a student has completed the full honours degree course but has not obtained the total required passes sufficient to merit a third-class honours degree. Alternatively a student may be denied honours if he/she has had to retake courses. An ordinary degree usually requires 300 CATS points whereas an honours degree requires 360 CATS points. It is possible to be awarded an ordinary degree with distinction if the average of the 300 CATS points is 70%+.

For a detailed explanation of the classification system see British undergraduate degree classification.

Ordinary degrees are unclassified degrees awarded to all students who have completed the course and obtained sufficient marks to pass the final assessments and examinations. Ordinary degree courses usually have lower entry requirements than Honours degree courses. Although Ordinary degree courses are often considered to be easier than Honours degree courses, this is not always the case, and much depends on the university attended and the subject being studied. Some modern universities offer the opportunity for Ordinary degree students to transfer to an Honours degree course in the same subject if an acceptable standard is reached after the first or second year of study.

Scotland

At the four Ancient universities of Scotland (St Andrews, Edinburgh, Glasgow and Aberdeen) and also at Dundee, undergraduate degrees are differentiated as either *Designated Degrees* or *Honours Degrees*.

An Honours degree (Master of Arts MA [Hons] for arts and social sciences or BSc [Hons] for sciences) is awarded for students who have completed four years at university - two years at *sub-honours* level, studying a variety of different subjects, and two years at *honours* level studying one subject in depth, usually including a dissertation in the final year. Honours degrees are further subdivided in classes. These are first class, upper second class (2:1) and lower second class (2:2).

A *designated degree* (MA or BSc) is awarded to students who have completed three years at university studying a variety of related subjects. The first two years of both a *Designated Degree* and an *Honours Degree* are identical, but candidates for the *Designated Degree* study in less depth in their final year, and often over a wider variety of subjects. Candidates for the *Designated Degree* do not usually complete a dissertation. A Scottish *Designated Degree* is different from an English *Pass Degree* even though both are denoted *BSc* Bachelor of Science.

United States

Many United States universities and colleges award bachelor's degrees with latin honors, usually (in ascending order) *cum laude* 'with honor/praise,' *magna cum laude* 'with great honor/praise,' the occasionally seen *maxima cum laude* 'with maximal honor/praise,' and *summa cum laude* 'with highest honor/praise.' Degrees without honors are awarded *rite*. Requirements for such notations of honors generally include minimum grade point averages (GPA), with the highest average required for the *summa* distinction. In the case of a few schools, a senior thesis for degrees in the humanities or laboratory research for natural science (and sometimes social science) degrees is also required. A notable exception is the Massachusetts Institute of Technology, which does not have a dean's list, Latin honors recognition, or undergraduate honors programme or subjects.

Bachelor's degrees in the United States are typically designed to be completed in four years of full-time study, although some programmes (such as engineering or architecture) usually take five, and some universities and colleges allow ambitious students (usually with the help of summer school and/or high school Advanced Placement courses) to complete them in as little as three years. Some U.S. colleges and universities have a separate academic track known as an "honors" or "scholars" program, generally offered to the top percentile of students (based on GPA), that offers more challenging courses or more individually-directed seminars or research projects in lieu of the standard core curriculum. The students are awarded the same bachelor's degree as students completing the standard curriculum, but with the notation *in cursu honorum* on the transcript and the diploma. Usually, the above Latin honors are separate from the notation for this honors course, but a student in the honors course generally must maintain grades worthy of at least the *cum laude* notation anyway. Hence, a graduate might receive a diploma *Artium Baccalaureatum rite* or *Artium Baccalaureatum summa cum laude* in the regular course or *Artium Baccalaureatum summa cum laude in cursu honorum* in the honors course.

If the student has completed the requirements for an honors degree only in a particular discipline (e.g., English language and literature), the degree is designated accordingly (e.g., BA with Honors in English). In this case, the degree candidate will complete the normal curriculum for all subjects except the selected discipline ("English," in the preceding example). The requirements in either case usually require completion of particular honors seminars, independent research at a level higher than usually required (often with greater personal supervision by faculty than usual), and a written honors thesis in the major subject.

English-Speaking World

New Bachelor's Degrees

The Universities of Oxford and Cambridge are perhaps alone in the United Kingdom today in awarding the BA for all undergraduate degrees. Almost all American universities award both BA and BS degrees, though a number of small liberal arts colleges award only the BA. However, on a global scale, many universities over the last hundred years have expanded the range of bachelor's degrees enormously, especially in countries such as Australia, New Zealand,

Pakistan, India, and South Africa. This represents a move towards specialization in tertiary education, in which college or university in these countries is intended to be a training for a specific career, and therefore akin to vocational education. It is a departure from the liberal arts approach common in the United States, in which the graduate is versed in a wide variety of subjects in addition to an academic major with the intent they be well prepared to pursue any number of careers or a progression of careers.

A full list of British degree abbreviations is also available.

BA, AB, BS, BAAS, BSc, SB, ScB

Today, the most common undergraduate degrees given are the Bachelor of Arts (*Artium Baccalaureus*) (BA, AB) and the Bachelor of Science (*Scientiæ Baccalaureus*) (BS, BSc, SB, ScB). Originally, in the universities of Oxford, Cambridge and Dublin, all undergraduate degrees were in the Faculty of Arts, hence the degree of Bachelor of Arts. The Bachelor of Applied Arts and Sciences (BAAS) is an undergraduate degree that bridges academic and work-life experiences.

Since the late 19th century, most universities in the Commonwealth have followed the practice of the University of London in dividing undergraduate degree subjects other than Law, Medicine, and Engineering, into the two broad categories of arts and sciences; conferring the degree of Bachelor of Arts upon students of the former and admitting students of the latter to the degree of Bachelor of Science.

In the United States, many colleges (particularly liberal arts colleges) as well as universities award the Bachelor of Arts for all academic (non pre-professional) subjects. In these institutions, students studying academic subjects

(English, chemistry, etc.) would receive a Bachelor of Arts while students studying for professions (police science, finance, nursing) would receive a Bachelor of Sciences. Some schools award the Bachelor of Arts for the humanities and the Bachelor of Sciences for both natural sciences and social sciences. In some cases a student may choose between a BA course of study and a BS course of study in the same subject at the same college.

Three American universities—the California Institute of Technology, the Georgia Institute of Technology, and the Massachusetts Institute of Technology—as well as the five United States Service academies—the Military, Naval, Air Force, Merchant Marine, and Coast Guard Academies—award the Bachelor of Science for all subjects, including subjects that at other institutions would be awarded a Bachelor of Arts (such as literature). Harvard University, on the other hand, offers only the degrees "Bachelor of Arts" and "Bachelor of Liberal Arts" except to engineering students who may be award an SB in engineering as a supplement to the Bachelor of Arts, which still must be earned first.

BA Econ, BEc, BEconSc, BSc(Econ)

The Bachelor of Economics is a degree awarded to students who have completed a course of study in the field of economics. Courses typically last three years, but may last as long as six.

BEng, BE, BSE, BAI, BIng, BESc, BASc, BTech, BSc(Eng)

The Bachelor of Engineering (*Baccalaureus in Arte Ingeniaria*) degree or the Bachelor of Applied Science degree is a professional degree awarded to students who have completed the three or four year course of study in engineering. There are more specific variants for many subfields, such as the BSEE degree (*Bachelor of Science in Electrical Engineering*). The BAI is awarded by the University of Dublin (Trinity College Dublin). The BSE (Bachelor of Software Engineering) is awarded by the University of Waterloo. Some South African Universities refer to their Engineering degrees as BIng (Baccalaureus Ingeniaria) .

In India BE is awarded in specific discipline such as computers, electrical, electronics, mechanical, communication, civil, plastics, chemical etc. Specialization is referred into brackets i.e. "BE(computers)".

BCom

The Bachelor of Commerce (BCom, or BComm in Canada) is an undergraduate degree in finance, business management, accounting and economic fields. The degree is also known as the Bachelor of Commerce and Administration (BCA).

BComn

The Bachelor of Communication (BComn) is an undergraduate degree in communication studies.

BComp, BCompSc, BIT, BInfTech, BAppSci (IT)

The Bachelor of Computing (BComp), Bachelor of Computer Science (BCompSc), Bachelor of Information Technology (BIT/BInfTech/BInfoTech), Bachelor of Applied Science (Information Technology) (BAppSc(IT)), are all undergraduate degrees in Information Technology often incorporating various aspects like programming, database design, software engineering, networks and information systems to prepare graduates for further postgraduate research degrees or employment in any variety of roles in the Information Technology industry.

BSET

The Bachelor of Science in Engineering Technology degree is a professional degree awarded to students who have completed a four year course of study in engineering technology. There are variants including general engineering technology, mechanical engineering technology, electrical engineering technology and civil engineering technology. Some of these variants even have optional areas of concentration. For instance mechanical engineering technology could include mechanical systems design, manufacturing systems, marine engineering technology, among others.

BArch

The Bachelor of Architecture is a professional degree awarded to students who complete the five year course of study in the field.

BAvn

The Bachelor of Aviation is awarded to students who complete a four year course of study in the field.

BBA, BSBA, BSB

The Bachelor of Business Administration, Bachelor of Science in Business Administration, or Bachelor of Science in Business is awarded to students who complete three to four years of full-time study in business administration. Such degrees often involve majors in a specific field such as accounting, finance, marketing, management, management information systems, HRM/personnel, strategic management, etc.

BBIS

The Bachelor of Business Information Systems is a degree which combines IT with business study. In some institutions, this is a professionally orientated degree. As with most other bachelors degrees, the BBIS is usually awarded after 3-4 years of full time study.

BD, BTh, BRS, BBS, BRE

The Bachelor of Divinity, Bachelor of Theology, Bachelor of Religious Studies, Bachelor of Biblical Studies or Bachelor of Religious Education is awarded upon completion of a programme of study of divinity or related disciplines, such as theology, religious studies, or religious education. In some universities it is a first degree, in others it is a higher degree. While it is generally conferred upon completion of a four-year program, it is also conferred in some specialized three-year programmes. From there the next level of advancement is generally the Master of Divinity, Master of Theology, Master of Religious Studies, or Master of Religious Education.

[BDes

The Bachelor of Design is awarded to those who complete the four years course of study in design, usually majoring in a specific field of design.

BDent

The Bachelor of Dentistry is the degree awarded exclusively from the University of Sydney Faculty of Dentistry in Sydney, Australia. This four year degree requires a previous bachelor's degree (minimum three years) and is the only one of its kind in Australia. When dentistry at the University of Sydney was an undergraduate course (pre-2001) the degree awarded was a Bachelor of Dental Surgery and is still in use at other dental schools across Australia.

BFA

The Bachelor of Fine Arts is a specialized degree awarded for courses of study in the fine and/or performing arts, frequently by an arts school or conservatory, although it is equally available at a significant number of traditional colleges and universities. In contrast to the BA or BS, which are generally considered to be academic degrees, the BFA is usually referred to as a professional degree, whose recipients have generally received four years of study and training in their major field, as compared to the two years of study in the major field usually found in most traditional non-Commonwealth Bachelor of Arts or Bachelor of Science programmes.

BF&TV

The Bachelor of Film and Television is an undergraduate degree for the study of film and/or television production including areas of cinematography, directing, scriptwriting, sound, animation and typography.

BIS

The Bachelor of Integrated Studies is an interdisciplinary bachelor's degree offered by several universities in the United States and Canada that allows students to design a customized and specific course of study to best suit their educational and professional objectives. Generally, this degree is sponsored by two or more departments within the university. Schools which confer the BIS degree include Pittsburg State University, Weber State University, Ferris State University, Arizona State University, University of Minnesota, and the University of New Brunswick, among others.

BJ, BAJ, BSJ

The Bachelor of Journalism degree is a professional degree awarded to students who have studied journalism at a four-year accredited university. Not all universities, however, grant this degree. In the United States, schools tend to offer the BA or BS with a major in journalism instead. The world's oldest school of journalism at the University of Missouri offers a BJ degree, not to be confused with the Bachelor degree in Jurisprudence at Oxford University.

BKin, BPE, BHK, BHPE, BSc(Kin)

The Bachelor of Kinesiology degree is specialized degree in the field of human movement and kinetics. Some schools still offer it under the aegis of a School of Physical Education (BPE or BHPE), although "kinesiology" or "human kinetics" is currently the more popular accepted term for the discipline.

BLArch

The Bachelor of Landscape Architecture is awarded to students who complete the five year course of study in the field.

BLA, ABL, BGS, BSGS, BAS, BPS

The Bachelor of Liberal Arts, Bachelor of General Studies, Bachelor of Liberal Studies, Bachelor of Science in General Studies or Bachelor of Applied Studies is sometimes awarded to students who major in the liberal arts, general, or interdisciplinary studies. The Bachelor of Professional Studies is awarded to students who major in professional career studies.

BLS, BLib, BLIS

The Bachelor of Library Science or Bachelor of Library

and Information Science is sometimes awarded to students who major in library science.

BMedSc, BBiomedSc, BMedSci

The title BMedSc is granted to students who have qualified in the field of biomedical science and medical science. Such universities that offer this course are the University of Birmingham in the UK and the University of New South Wales, the University of Queensland, the University of Sydney, Flinders University, Griffith University, Monash University, Australian National University and the University of Melbourne in Australia. The degree of BMedSci may also be awarded to an individual who, having followed the prescribed course of study for the degrees of MB ChB/MB BS, does not complete their undergraduate clinical training. In brief, this is normally awarded having completed successfully the first three years of an undergraduate medical degree at certain UK medical institutions.

BAOM

The Bachelor of Arts in Organizational Management is awarded to students who complete a four year course of study in the field. The core functions of this programme are to learn organizational functions, communication, group behavior, decision making, human resource management, ethics, and to develop and deploy effective skills in management and leadership.

BM or BMus

The Bachelor of Music degree is a professional or academic undergraduate degree in music at most conservatories in the U.S. It is also commonly awarded at schools of music in large private or public universities.

Areas of study typically include music performance, music education, music composition, academic fields (music history/ musicology, music theory, ethnomusicology), and may include jazz, commercial music, recording technology, sacred music/ music ministry, or music business. Small liberal arts colleges and universities without schools of music often award only BAs in music, with different sets of requirements. (see also: *BFA*)

BN, BNSc, BScN, BSN, BNurs

The Bachelor of Nursing Science (BNSc or BScN) or Bachelor of Nursing (BN) is a three- to four-year undergraduate degree that prepares students for a career in nursing, subject to completion of exams in their area of residence to gain "registered nurse" status. Sometimes referred to as BSN or Bachelor of Science in Nursing.

BPharm

The Bachelor of Pharmacy was the principal academic degree for the practice of pharmacy in the United States. However, most colleges of pharmacy have phased out the degree in favor of the PharmD, or Doctor of Pharmacy, degree.

BPhil, PhB

The Bachelor of Philosophy degree is either an undergraduate or graduate degree. Generally, it entails independent research or a thesis/capstone project.

BAPSY, BSc(Psych)

The Bachelor of Arts or Science in Psychology is a degree awarded to students who have completed a course of study in the field of psychology. Courses typically last three years, but may last as long as six. In Nepal there are three- and four-year course available for higher-level students.

BSE, BS in Ed

The Bachelor of Science in Education is a four-year undergraduate degree offered by many US colleges and universities for those preparing to be licensed as teachers. Variants include the BEd, BA Ed, BAT (Bachelor of Arts for Teaching), and BST. Preparatory to the MS in Ed, this degree is most often taken by those interested in early childhood, elementary level, and special education, or by those planning to be school administrators. Secondary level teachers often major in their subject area instead (such as history, chemistry, or mathematics), with a minor in education.

BSc Ed

The Bachelor of Science and/with Education is a degree awarded to students who complete the four- to five-year course of study in the field of science (major and minor in biology, chemistry, physics, math) and education. Although notionally BSc and BEd are two degrees, they must be taken together.

BSPH

The Bachelor of Science in Public Health is a four year undergraduate degree that prepares students for careers in the public, private, or non-profit sector in areas such as public health, environmental health, health administration, epidemiology, or health policy and planning.

BSL

The Bachelor of Science in Law is a special-purpose degree that allows someone who has had some prior studies but has not achieved a bachelor's degree to resume their education and pursue the study of law towards an eventual Juris Doctor degree.

BSocSc

The Bachelor of Social Science is a three or four year undergraduate British degree that enables students to specialize in the area of social science. Compared to the Bachelor of Arts, which allows students to study a vast range of disciplines, the Bachelor of Social Science enables students to develop more central and specialized knowledge of the social sciences. Many universities place the Bachelor of Social Science between the Bachelor of Arts and Bachelor of Science undergraduate degrees.

BVSc, BVMS, BVM&S

The Bachelor of Veterinary Science is a five-year course of study that is generally required for becoming a veterinarian. It is also known as the Bachelor of Veterinary Medicine and Surgery at some universities.

LLB

The Bachelor of Laws is the principal academic degree in law in most common law countries other than the United States, where it has been superseded by the doctorate level Juris Doctor degree.

BMath

The Bachelor of Mathematics degree is awarded by the University of Waterloo. It is offered as a 4 year honors programme or a 3 year general programme. Several other universities, mostly in Canada and Australia, also award Bachelor of Mathematics degrees.

Other

There are many other specialised bachelor's degrees offered. Some are in very specialised areas, like the five-year BID or BSID degree in industrial design. Others are offered only at a limited number of universities, such as the Walsh School of Foreign Service at Georgetown University's Bachelor of Science in Foreign Service (BSFS). The University of Delaware offers a Bachelor's of Applied Arts and Science (BAAS) degree for many majors within their school of Arts and Science, which often indicate an interdisciplinary course of study. Stanford University's BAS (Bachelor of Arts and Sciences) degree is for students completing two Arts and Sciences majors, one of which would ordinarily lead to the BA while the other would ordinarily lead to the BS, but who are receiving only one degree.

At many institutions one can only complete a two-degree programme if the bachelor's degrees to be earned are of different types, e.g., one could earn a BA in philosophy and a BS ChE in chemical engineering simultaneously, but a person studying philosophy and English would receive only a single BA with the two majors. Rules on this vary considerably, however.

Asia Pacific

The education systems in Asian countries are largely patterned after the western models.

Australia

In Australia the award of Honours is given to students who have achieved a higher level of performance in a fourth additional year to a typical Bachelor degree. Some bachelor degrees have inclusive Honours as part of a four year degree (such as engineering). This Honours year consists generally of half coursework units and half thesis. Honours is generally for those who want to take up a research track for postgraduate studies. Differing between universities is the marking scale for Honours. Generally 65 - 75(Third class), 75 - 85 (second class (broken down into A and B or First Division and Second Division), 85+ (First class). First class and Second class First division is generally the standard required for entry into a PhD or Masters by Research in Australia.

Bangladesh

In Bangladesh, Universities and Colleges award three and four years degree in Science (BS, BSc, BCS, BBA, BBIT ,BCom etc.) and two to four years degree in Arts (BA, BCom, etc.). Engineering Universities provided 4 years degree programme for bachelor's. Medical colleges have 5 year degree programme. In law education there is 3 years LLB degree after 2 years of BA, so total 5 years study. All of these programmes begin after achieving Higher Secondary Certificate (HSC - in total 12 years of education).

Eligibility : 50% 12th (science) / You can go for degree after diploma engineering(direct 2nd year intake)

China

Since the undergraduate education system in China is modeled after its American counterpart, all the degrees are adapted from those of the United States. Thus four years education is almost a standard length, although some private small colleges do offer 3 year programmes, which cannot award a degree credentialed by education bureau. Normally, about 90% graduates can obtain a degree, however, no degree is awarded with excellency or honor. It is also referred as a "xueshi" (f[ëX).

India

In India, arts, commerce and science colleges provide three year bachelor's degrees (BA, BSc, BBA, BCA, BCom, etc.). Generally these programmes are of three years duration and begin after secondary school year 12. After successful completion of these programmes, a Bachelor's degree is awarded by the respective university to which the college is affiliated.

Engineering and medical colleges provide 4 to 5 years degree programmes for bachelor's degree (BE, BArch, BTech, MBBS) that also begin after secondary school year 12(also called +2). The Bachelor of Architecture (BArch) degree programme is of 5 years duration.

Japan

Institutes of higher learning in Japan provide four years of college education leading to a bachelor's degree which is referred to as "*gakushi* e.g., Gakushi in Economics. Some institutes offer six-year programmes leading to a professional degree.

Malaysia

Institutes of higher learning in Malaysia provides three or four years of education leading to a BSc Hons Degree. There are also twinning programmes with Australian and UK universities.

New Zealand

In New Zealand, only recognised institutions — usually universities — have degree awarding powers.

Most bachelor's degrees are three years full time, but certain degrees such as the Bachelor of Laws and the Bachelor of Engineering require four years of study. A Bachelor of Medicine requires a minimum of six years.

Where students opt to study two bachelor's degrees simultaneously — referred to as a 'conjoint degree' or 'double degree' — an extra year of study is added. The number of years of study required is determined based on the degree with the greatest number of years. For example, a Bcom degree requires three years of full-time study, but a conjoint Bcom-LLB degree will require five years of full-time study because the LLB degree is four years long. Exceptional students may choose to complete a degree in a shorter amount of time by taking on extra courses, and usually with the help of summer school. Students who complete a conjoint degree programme will have two separate bachelor's degrees at the end of their studies.

Consistently high-performing students may also be invited to complete the 'Honours' programme. This usually requires an extra year of study with an extra Honours thesis. An Honours award is credited with 'Hons.', for example, 'Bachelor of Laws (Hons.)'.

Pakistan

In Pakistan, arts, commerce and science colleges provide four year bachelor's degrees (BA, BSc, BBA, BCom, etc.). Generally these programmes are of four years duration and begin after secondary school year 12. After successful completion of these programmes, a Bachelor's degree is awarded by the respective university to which the college is affiliated. Generally BCom & BA are for two years and could be enrolled as external candidate (external candidate are enroll for examination & study programme on self basis or through private tution providers). Main university offering these two programmes is University of Karachi where more than 10,000 students appears in BA & BCom exam as external candidate.

Engineering and medical colleges provide 4 and 5 year degree programmes respectively for bachelor's degree (BE, BArch, BTech begin after 3 year Diploma of Associate Engineer, MBBS) that also begin after secondary school year 12. BTech(Hon's) degree is at par and compatible to BE/BSc Engineering. The Bachelor of Architecture (BArch) degree programme is of 5 years duration

Philippines

In the Philippines, where the term "course" is commonly used to refer to a bachelor's degree major, course of study or program, several undergraduate categories exist - the two most common degrees awarded being Bachelor of Science (BS) and Bachelor of Arts (AB or BA). Specializations ("majors") in economics, business administration, accountancy, radiologic technology, nursing, architecture and engineering fall under Science in most colleges and universities. The latter two specializations require five years of schooling, in contrast to the standard of four years. Other common degrees are Bachelor in Education (BEd), and Bachelor of Laws (LLB, a graduate degree). Being patterned after the United States, all universities and colleges offer graduation with honors - cum laude, magna cum laude, and summa cum laude.

Republic of Korea

Universities, colleges and institution of higher learning provide a bachelor's degree, called 'haksa' (Korean: YÕ¬À). For example, a university graduate student having majored in literature obtains BA, called 'munhaksa' (Korean: 8»YÕ¬À). Even if not going to educational institutes, people can get a bachelor's degree through Bachelor's Degree Examination for Self-Education.

Sri Lanka

In Sri Lanka, only recognised institutes of higher learning have degree awarding powers. There are bachelor's degrees that are three years full time with out a area of specialization, known as a "general degree". Degree's with a specialization (in Engineering, IT, Law, etc) known as a "spical degree" require four years of study and more entrance qualifications. A Degree in Medicine, a MBBS requires a minimum of six years.

Europe

Bachelor's degrees exist in almost every country in Europe. However, these degrees were only recently introduced in some Continental European countries, where Bachelor's degrees were unknown before the Bologna process.

Austria

The historical situation in Austria is very similar to the situation in Germany. The traditional first degrees are also the *Magister* and the *Diplom*. A new piece of educational legislation in 2002 reintroduced the Bachelors degree (awarded after three years) also in Austria.

Belgium

Since the new European system Bologna process, the 3 years Bachelor cursus replaces the old 3 years grad school which was called "graduat" or the old 2 or 3 years "candidatures" which prepare for university diploma.

Denmark

The Bachelor degree was re-introduced at universities in Denmark in 1993, after the original degree baccalaureus was abandoned in 1775. The bachelor degree is awarded after 3 or 4 years of study at a university, and follows a scheme much similar to the British one. Two bachelor degrees are used at university level today:

- *Bachelor of Science* (*BSc*), awarded to students with main focus on scientific, medical or technical areas.
- *Bachelor of Arts* (*BA*), awarded to students with main focus on humanistic, theological or jurisprudence areas.

The bachelor degree has also been used since the late 1990s in a number of areas like nursing and teaching. Usually referred to as a *profession-bachelor* these degrees usually requires 4 years of study at a college. These bachelor degrees do not grant automatic access to a university master's program, as opposed to the traditional bachelor degrees awarded by universities.

France

The traditional bachelor's degree is the equivalent of the French "Licence" 3 years degree. Since the new European system of 2004 "LMD" Bologna process was founded, it has become standard to recognise a Bachelor's over three years, a Master's over two years and a doctorate over three.

Germany

Bachelor's degrees, called *Bakkalaureus*, originally existed in Germany, but were abolished up until 1820 as part of educational reforms at this time. The Magister degree, originally a graduate degree, became the new first degree after five years of study. In 1899 a second first degree, the Diplom, was introduced when the *Technische Hochschulen* received university status.

However, in 1998 a new educational law reintroduced the Bachelor's degree (first degree after 3 years of study) in Germany. Today these degrees can be called either

Bakkalaureus or *Bachelor* (in accordance with federal law) but the English term is more common. The traditional degrees will be abolished by 2010.

Italy

Since the Bologna Process the old Italian five years laurea system is no longer in use. The BA level corresponds today to the "Laurea" (its name has been "Laurea Triennale" for a short time after reform), which has a normative time to completion of three years (notice that in Italy students graduate from high school at the age of 19) and grants the access to postgraduate degrees (the equivalent of Master Degree being "Laurea Magistrale", even though its name after reform has been "Laurea Specialistica" for a short time). In order to graduate, students must complete 180 credits and write a thesis. Graduation marks go from 66 to 110 (for some important Universities such as Polytechnics the maximum mark awarded is 100). According to each faculty internal ruling a *lode* (distinction) may be assigned to candidates with a 110/110 mark for recognition of the excellence of the thesis. BA/BSc and MA/MSc graduates in Italy are addressed as *Dottore* (for a man) or *Dottoressa* (for a woman).

Netherlands

In 2003/2004, the Dutch degree system was changed to abide to international standards. Former degrees such as the *baccalaureus* (bc. for Bachelor), *doctorandus* (prefix abbreviated to drs.; it corresponds to MA or MSc), *ingenieur* (ing. for those having graduated from a university of applied science after 4 years and ir. for those having graduated from university after 5 years), *meester in de rechten* (mr.; it corresponds to LL.M.) and *doctor* (dr.; it corresponds to Ph.D) are still granted along with their international equivalents.

Bachelor's degrees are granted by both accredited colleges and universities. For colleges after four years of education a bachelor's degree is obtained (e.g. BCom, BEng but no BA or BSc). For universities (incl. the honours liberal arts colleges which are locally called *university college*) after three years of education a degree is granted (BA, BSc and LLB)

Whether a bachelor's degree is granted by a college or university makes a lot of difference. BAs from a university grant 'immediate' entry into a master's programme (and are usually considered a formality to allow students entering foreign universities master's programmes), bachelor degrees from a college require an extra 'bridge year' (often called a 'pre-master' year) to be allowed into a master's programme, since university bachelors are already tutored in research fields, whereas college bachelors are not. Granted degrees may be used as suffixes (Jan Jansen BSc). Note: the English prefix 'Mr.' corresponds in Dutch with the official, and protected prefix 'mr.', meaning a 'meester in de rechten', i.e. a Master of Law, or the English equivalent LL.M.

Many Dutch universities have recently started offering Honours programmes / tracks to extra talented students. These are in some cases e.g. University College Utrecht, Utrecht Law College, University College Maastricht called *colleges* but are nevertheless types of university education.

Poland

In Poland, the licentiate degree corresponds to the Bachelor's degree in Anglophone countries.

Portugal

Presently the Portuguese equivalent of a bachelor's degree is the *licenciatura*, awarded after three years of study at an accredited university or polytechnical institution.

It is an undergraduate 1st study cycle programme which is required to advance into further studies like master's degree programmes. Before the Bologna Process (2006/2007) in Portuguese higher education, a *licenciatura* referred to a licentiate degree, which was a major bachelor's degree with professional accreditation, was five years of study (equivalent to the present bachelors plus the masters) but it was changed due to the European uniformization of scholarship degrees.

Russia and Ukraine

The specialist degree (Russian: ñïåöèàëèñò) was the first academic distinction in the Soviet Union. In the early 1990s, *Bakalavr* (Bachelor's) degrees were introduced in all the countries of the Commonwealth of Independent States, except Turkmenistan. After Bakalavr degree, one can earn a Master's degree (another 1–2 years) while preserving the old 5-year Specialist scheme. *Specialist* degree is now being discontinued in universities that take part in Bologna process, so new students don't have this option.

Spain

In Spain the equivalent to a bachelor's degree is called a "licenciatura". In accordance with the Bolonia Agreement, degrees are generally awarded after four or five years of study. The licenciatura, like the BA/BSc, is normally the prerequisite for graduate studies.

Sweden

The Swedish equivalent of a Bachelor's degree is the *kandidatexamen*. It is awarded after three years of study: a year and a half in the major subject and a year and a half in other subjects. A thesis equivalent to 15 ECTS credits must be included in the degree. The exception to this system is Theology, where a *teologie kandidat* (Bachelor of

Theology) is a four-year degree, equivalent to a Master's. Previously, there was a Bachelor of Law degree (*juris kandidat*) which contained 4.5 years of study, but this degree has now changed its name to *juristexamen* ("law degree").

Switzerland

Similarly to Austria and Germany, Switzerland does not have a tradition of Bachelor degrees. The traditional first degrees were the Licentiate and the Diplom and the second degrees were the DEA and the postgraduate diploma. Bachelor's and graduate Master's degrees replaced the old degrees in 2003 after the application of Bologna process.

Bachelor of Medicine and Bachelor of Surgery

In countries following British tradition, (the University of Malta is an exception) medical students pursue an undergraduate medical education and receive Bachelors degrees in Medicine and Surgery (MB BChir or BM BCh or BM BS or MB ChB or MB BS).

This was historically taken at the universities of Oxford, Cambridge and Dublin after the initial BA degree, and in Oxford, Cambridge and Dublin the BA is still awarded for the initial three years of medical study, with the BM BCh, MB BChir or MB BCh BAO respectively being awarded for the subsequent clinical stage of training. Some British universities give a bachelor's degree in science, or medical science, mid-way through the medical course, and most allow students to intercalate a year of more specialised study for a Bachelor of Science (BSc), Bachelor of Medical Science (BMedSci) or Bachelor of Medical Biology (BMedBiol) degree with honours.

Although notionally MB and BS are two degrees, they must be taken together, and by convention entitle the bearer to use the title of *Doctor*. In some Irish universities a third degree, Bachelor of Obstetrics (BAO), is added. However, this third degree is an anachronism from the 19th century and is not registerable with the Irish Medical Council.

The non-university (licentiate) qualifications allowing registration as a medical practitioner in the UK, which have not been awarded by the United Examining Board since 1999, also conferred the courtesy title of "doctor."

MASTER OF SOCIAL WORK

The Master of Social Work (MSW) is a master's degree in social work.

In the United States, M.SW degrees must be received from a graduate school that has been approved by the Council on Social Work Education (CSWE). The MSW requires two years of graduate study, in combination with two years' internship, also called field experience. While some students obtain a Bachelor of Social Work (BSW) before pursuing a Master's, most MSW programmes accept applicants with undergraduate degrees in a broad range of liberal arts degrees.

Most MSW programmes allow students to choose a clinical track, which focuses on direct practice with clients, or a community practice track, with a focus on political advocacy, community organizing, policy analysis and/or human services management. While the clinical track tends to be more popular, there has been a resurgence in community practice concentrations recently. There are also opportunities at many universities to obtain joint degrees, such as an MSW and a Public Administration degree, MSW and Public Health, or MSW and Law. The MSW practice scope has broadened in recent years to include the specialty practice areas of geriatrics and veterinary social work.

The MSW is considered a terminal degree in the field of clinical social work. The DSW (Doctorate of Social Work) or Ph.D in social work are the final degrees offered in the field of social work. The DSW is considered the professional doctoral degree, while the Ph.D in social work is viewed as the research or academic doctoral degree.

Though Master of Social Work is by far the most common degree title used by graduate social work schools in the United States, it is not universal. For example, Columbia University School of Social Work offers an M.S. degree in social work, the School of Social Service Administration of the University of Chicago confers an A.M. degree, and both the University of Texas and the University of Wisconsin-Madison confer the MSSW (Master of Science in Social Work) degree. The Mandel School of Applied Social Sciences at Case Western Reserve University confers the MSSA (Master of Science in Social Administration) degree.

DOCTOR OF SOCIAL WORK

The Doctor of Social Work (DSW) is a professional, social work specific academic degree for experienced social work practitioners who wish to further their careers by gaining doctoral level education and training in advanced practice, teaching and supervision, research and/or policy analysis. Much of the course work emphasizes practice issues, education in social work, research and qualitative and quantitative analysis methods. The degree typically leads to teaching, research, leadership roles, or in self-employed clinical social work practice.

The DSW degree was originally designed to be a professional practice degree, similar to practice degrees in other professions such as the M.D., that was specific to the social work profession. Much of the course work now is similar to that offered in Ph.D. programmes, and includes a doctoral candidacy examination, after the completion of the required coursework, prior to being eligible to start on the dissertation research.. The DSW has become less popular in the past several decades, as most of the Schools of Social Work now offer only Ph.D. programmes in social work. There has been the movement to retroactively change DSWs to Ph.D.s in a few programmes; however, the DSW is still a recognized within the profession. The doctoral degrees are offered within CSWE accredited university programmes focused both on the MSW and doctoral degrees.

INTERNATIONAL ASSOCIATION OF SCHOOLS OF SOCIAL WORK

The International Association of Schools of Social Work (IASSW) is the international association of schools of social work and other institutions of learning. The IASSW promotes the development of social work education throughout the world, develops standards to enhance quality of social work education, encourages international exchange, provides forums for sharing social work research and scholarship, and promotes human rights and social development through policy and advocacy activities. They also work in a consultative role with the United Nations. They host a biennial conference of social work educators called the IASSW Congress and publish a newsletter.

The IASSW was founded in 1928 at the First International Conference of Social Work, held in Paris. It initially comprised 51 schools, mostly in Europe, and was known as the International Committee. Revitalized after World War II, the organization expanded its membership to include a wider range of countries and was renamed the

International Association of Schools of Social Work. The association has member schools in all parts of the world; 5 regional organizations in Africa; Asia and the Pacific; Europe; Latin America; and North America and the Caribbean are affiliated with the IASSW and represented on the Board of Directors.

Professor Janice Wood Wetzel is the main representative.

COUNCIL ON SOCIAL WORK EDUCATION

The Council on Social Work Education (CSWE) is the premiere association for

CSWE has a number of educational programmes designed to improve the quality of education for social workers, and holds its Annual Programme Meeting each year as a place where all can convene to strengthen the profession. It also sets and maintains standards of courses and accreditation of bachelor's degree's and Master's degree programmes in social work.

The CSWE specifies foundation social work programme components, but social work specialties areas are defined by the individual accredited MSW programmes. "Social work education is grounded in the liberal arts and contains a coherent, integrated professional foundation in social work practice from which an advanced practice curriculum is built at the graduate level." (CSWE, Educational Programmes and Accreditation Standards).

For a list of BSW and MSW programmes accredited by the Council, visit their web site.

HIGHER EDUCATION AND TRAINING FOR SOCIAL WORK

The first paper traces the historical growth of higher

education, the second examines the diffusion of American social work education in India, and the last one focuses on the dilemmas of social work education.

One of the major themes which has been emphasised relates to the need for indigenous foundations of Indian educational system. In the past thirty years, several Commissions, Committees and Study Groups have examined the educational system and have struck the same note in their reports. Ironically, little progress has been made to develop indigenous study material for the benefit of students. Centres of scholarship and national institutes of training which have been established in recent years continue to derive inspiration and nourishment from foreign scholars, universities and literature. Most of the higher education as exists is found to be irrelevant to the needs of Indian culture and society, and has increasingly become dysfunctional. A case study of social work education is presented in this context.

Over the last three decades, there has been a considerable discussion about the restructuring of our educational objectives and organisations, but little has been done so far. Our educational system is still rooted more or less on the traditional British pattern. Unfortunately, it is forgotten that education is a socio-cultural product and must perform some necessary functions, if it has to become an effective instrument in the promotion of social and economic development. It is a sad story that the educational system, especially higher education continues to be dominated by Western philosophies, scholarship and textbooks. The need to cultivate pride in indigenous scholarship is long overdue.

Among the recent books which should be read with interest are those of Yogesh Atal, *Social Sciences, The*

Indian Scene (New Delhi, 1976); T. N. Dhar, *Education and Employment in India, The Policy Nexus* (Calcutta, 1977); M. S. Huq, *Education-Manpower and Development in South and South East Asia* (New Delhi, 1976): G. S. Mansukhani, *Crisis in Indian Universities* (New Delhi, 1972); A. Rama Murthy, *Restructuring the University*, (New Delhi, 1976); J. N. Kaul (ed.), *Higher Education, Social Change and National Development* (Simla, 1975); J. P. Naik, *Equality, Quality, and Quantity, Elusive Triangle in Indian Education,* (Bombay, 1975); P. Ramachandran, *Social Welfare Manpower in Greater Bombay* (Bombay, 1977); VKRV Rao, *Education and Human Resource Development* (New Delhi, 1966); S. and L. Rudolphs (ed.), *Education and Politics in India* (New Delhi, 1972); P. D. Shukla, *Towards the New Pattern of Education in India* (New Delhi, 1976) and D. D. Tiwari, *Thoughts on Education* (Allahabad, 1972).

As before, social work education continues to be under the influence of its counter-part in the United States. Some marginal modifications have, however, been made to promote indigenous study material. One of the most significant changes in the well-established system was introduced by Tata Institutes of Social Sciences by offering a separate master's programme in Personal Management and Industrial Relations. The Faculty of Social Work, University of Baroda, has developed a diploma course in Industrial Relations and Personnel Management. Several institutions including Tata Institute, Delhi Schools of Social Work and the Faculty of Social Work at Baroda have also established doctoral programmes in Social Work. The Department of Social Work, Lucknow University, and the Institute of Social Sciences, Agra University are among the oldest institutions which have been offering doctoral degrees in Social Work.

The Handbook on Social Work Education Facilities in India (New Delhi, 1976), a government publication, has fulfilled a long awaited need. According to this document, there are now 34 Schools of Social Work or Departments of Social work, of which 24 offer Master's degree, 10 Bachelor's degree courses, 2 M. Phil courses, and 11 doctoral programmes. The ecological spread of these institutions, however, remains uneven. More than half of our States (12 out of 22) have no institution offering any programme of Social Work training at the present time. Among them are included Arunachal Pradesh, Assam, Bihar, Haryana, Himachal Pradesh, Jammu- Kashmir, Orissa and Punjab.

In recent years, the Department of Social Welfare in the Ministry of Education and Social Welfare, Government of India has sponsored a series of studies to determine social welfare manpower requirements in different States. Of course, these studies will provide some valuable data. However, the basic problem is not the lack of data on needs and requirements which are generally obvious. But the fundamental issue which has been confronting both political leadership and academic community for almost three decades, has been to explore ways and means of converting the existing schools, departments and centres of social work training so as to meet the challenge of social problems on an indigenous basis. This goal still remains a far cry in wilderness and the Western model of social work education continues to survive unabated!

GROWTH OF HIGHER EDUCATION AND NEED FOR CULTURAL FOUNDATIONS

Higher education, in the modern sense of the word, is less than one hundred and fifty years old. It is true, however, that in the long history of the country, beginning thousands of years before the Christian Era, centres of learning had existed in one form or another. Ancient Nalanda and Taxila Universities have become synonymous with the highest achievements of education in early Indian history. But it is difficult to speak of nature of ancient Indian education with certainty, for our information is based on documents of unequal date and unequal value. We only know that a definite conception of higher education did exist and that there were some centres of higher learning in ancient India. While some of these centres in the eastern and southern parts of the country had continued their work throughout the middle ages, most of them had disappeared by then because of foreign invasions, religious persecutions and other historical vicissitudes. The Islamic rulers had introduced their culture and education by establishing some madrasahs (schools or colleges) in the middle ages which has continued to flourish till their power decayed and fell before the advancing tide of the British influence. Thus the universities of modern India owe very little to her ancient and medieval centres of learning and have arisen without any formal connection or continuity with the traditional institutions of higher learning.

Historical Survey of Higher Education

Up to the last decade of the eighteenth century, the British had not paid much attention to the introduction of Western education in Indian schools and colleges. In the year 1834, Lord Macaulay stated the case for the re-orientation of education and urged the government to undertake the promotion of European literature and science. Under the new system, started in 1835, education rapidly expanded, and English schools and colleges grew up in different parts of the country. The most important step towards the development of education was taken in 1854, as a result of which the Universities of Bombay, Calcutta and Madras were founded by the Act of Incorporation passed on January 24,, 1857. The Christian Missions, which were quite active in the eighteenth century in promoting some form of Western education, had in fact provided the initial impetus to the East India Company for encouraging and propagating Western education. By 1840, the various Missions had almost universally come to accept the view that the English education would lead to the spread of Christianity and, therefore, supported new educational policy. Generally speaking, the British attempted to maintain an overall policy of religious neutrality towards the existing institutions run by both Hindus and Muslims, and allowed the continued existence of the old classical schools side by side with the English schools. Perhaps encouragement to the native learning was intended and continued, but the vernacular schools, as they came to be called, fought a losing battle with the English schools in the years which followed.

The history of the first twenty-five years of university education was mainly one of growth in the number of students and of colleges affiliated to the three existing universities. Private colleges were encouraged as a matter of policy because, they cost the State less than the government colleges and were considered more efficient. The increase in number of candidates for the examinations and the vast extent of the area under the jurisdiction of the universities led to proposals for the establishment of new universities and new government colleges as well. The creation of the Punjab University (1882) and the Allahabad University (1887) was consistent with the universities established earlier as affiliating bodies, though they did accept the principle that the universities could take up teaching work through the appointment of university professors and lecturers. By 1946, the last year of British rule in India, the number of universities had grown to eighteen with about two thousand affiliated colleges attached to them. But there was no substantial change in the basic pattern of higher education which had somewhat crystallised by the beginning of the 20th century. Initially, the universities were not teaching bodies; they used to prescribe courses of study, conducted examinations and awarded diplomas to successful candidates. The actual teaching was done by colleges affiliated to the universities. These colleges were either government colleges or private colleges, and were largely free to adopt their own ways of teaching and to appoint their own staff. The administration of the universities was vested in the Senate, consisting of a Chancellor who held the formal position of a Governor of the Province or State, a Vice-Chancellor (who was the real head) and Fellows, which were nominated by the government and represented different branches of government. The Senate was to delegate its executive authority in a Syndicate, composed of the Vice-Chancellor and six Fellows elected by the four Faculties—Arts, Law, Medicine and Engineering. The Syndicate was to appoint members of the various Faculties, which in turn had to recommend examiners to the Syndicate for appointment. The day-to-day administration was entrusted to an official designated as Registrar who was appointed by the Vice-Chancellor. As a matter of fact this pattern continues to govern most of the Universities even today.

There is no denying the fact, however, that from time to time the British Government had appointed Commissions and Committees to inquire into the objectives, problems and prospects of the universities in order to formulate some basic principles of educational policy. Although the objectives were never clearly formulated, it became clear over the years that the two main objectives were to meet the urgent administrative needs of preparing natives for public employment, and to promote English literature and science among the Indian people. The rapidly increasing number of candidates, changing economic and political conditions and emerging political consciousness during the last decade of the nineteenth century and the early decades of the twentieth century necessitated readjustments of the educational system not only in terms of the universities, but also in their administration and curriculum planning. As a result of the recommendations of the Calcutta University Commission, constant attempts were made to liberalised constitutions of universities, to introduce new fields of study, to develop research facilities and to allow them a large amount of teaching activity on their own. But so long as the English system of education subserved the British political interests, no far-reaching changes were made in it. The "Seargent Report", prepared by the Government of India in 1944, viewed Indian education for the first time in the context of an awakened India during the British rule. But this plan was shelved and did not form the basis of national educational development when the Independence came along.

Post-Independence Developments

In the wake of enthusiasm that marked the attainment of Independence in 1947, there was a new awareness of the broader scope of responsibilities that the universities must have in a free country. It became necessary to inquire how far the existing system of higher education was adequate to meet the needs of the changed political conditions and in what ways the system needed to be altered and enlarged consistent with the cultural, social and economic conditions of the Country. Realising the urgency and importance of the role of higher education, the Government of India appointed the University Education Commission in November 1948, to report on Indian University education and to suggest improvements and extensions that might be desirable to suit present and future requirements. The report of the Commission, which was completed in August of 1949, was the first comprehensive attempt at reorganisation of higher education since Independence. The Commission observed that "We were everywhere struck by a deep general awareness of the importance of higher education for national welfare and an uneasy sense of the inadequacy of the present pattern. While it is generally recognised that the universities should provide the best teaching over the entire field of knowledge which its own resources may permit, they should offer this teaching to the widest range of students irrespective of class, sex, caste or religion, that they should extend, by original inquiry, the frontiers of learning and, above all mould and shape students not merely by the training of the intellect but by the disciplining of the spirit. The universities as the makers of the future cannot persist in the old patters, however valid they may have been' in their own way. With the increasing complexity of a society and its shifting patterns, universities have to change their objectives and methods, if they are to function effectively in our national life. A policy of drift in the vague hope that, if the universities are granted full autonomy and are permitted to pursue their own ends with intelligence and imagination, higher education will take care of itself, will be dangerous. Automatic and spontaneous adjustment will not take us to the future we want. We must develop a comprehensive positive policy within the limits of which there should be ample scope for pioneering and experimentation."

In subsequent years, the Government of India had accepted the recommendations of the Commission in principle, and several steps were taken to reorganise some aspects of the educational system. One of the most important of these steps was perhaps the creation of the University Grants Commission in November of 1953. The Commission was primarily empowered to make grants to universities for new developments. In consequence, it has gradually assumed responsibilities for the promotion, development and coordination of university education on the one hand and to determine, improve and maintain proper standards in teaching, examinations and research on the other. The Commission has over the years helped colleges and universities to upgrade their courses to the newly developed degree standards, to give their staff a higher scale of salaries, to build libraries, laboratories, hostels and to institute a system of scholarship and fellowship for the students whose performance is considered superior. Another recommendation of the Commission pertained to the establishment of rural universities for the spread of higher education in rural areas which was examined by a Committee on Rural Higher Education in 1954. As a result of their investigation, a new pattern under the name of rural institutes was accepted which started a three-year diploma course, and a two-year certificate course, the former being rated as equivalent to the bachelor's degree course of universities.

In September 1952, another Commission was appointed to examine the prevailing system of Secondary education in the country and to suggest measures for its reorganisation and improvement just as the University just as the University Education Commission had done for university education earlier. According to the Third Five Year Plan, the programme for the reorganisation and improvement of secondary education, which was taken up following the report of the Secondary Education Commission, had proceeded along several lines and was designed both to enlarge the content of secondary education and to make it a self-contained unit within the educational process. The measures which were taken related to the conversion of high schools into higher secondary schools, development of multipurpose schools with provision for a number of elective subjects along with and in addition to the academic courses, expansion and improvement of facilities for the teaching of science, provision, of educational and vocational guidance, improvement of the examination and evaluation system, enlargement of the facilities for vocational education, increased facilities for the education of girls and the backward classes and encouragement to merit scholarships. In the educational history of the country, the secondary stage of education was correctly defined in the Report of the Secondary Education Commission, for the first time, as a self-sufficient course preparing students to enter life after completing the course. Earlier their main objective has all along been considered as the preparation for the university, which has consequently dominated the schools more than any other single purpose. The fact, that for most students, formal education ends, or should end, with the high school, emphasises a clear-cut need for developing and reorganising the secondary education on new lines. Further, it has been increasingly realised that in the middle and lower levels of many branches of economic life, in administration, in rural development, in commerce, in industry and in the professions, the requirements of trained manpower have to be met by the products of secondary schools.

More than a decade ago, we saw another monumental report of the Education Commission, which was appointed in July 1964 and had completed its work in June 1966. The Commission observed, "Indian education needs a drastic reconstruction, almost a revolution. "We need to bring about major improvements in the effectiveness of primary education, to introduce work-experience as an integral part of general education; to vocationalise secondary education; to improve the quality of teachers in sufficient strength; to liquidate illiteracy; to strengthen centres of advanced study and strive to attain in some of our universities at least, higher international standards; to lay special emphasis on the combination of teaching and research; to pay particular attention to education and research in agriculture and allied sciences. All this calls for a determined and large-scale action. Tinkering with the existing situation, and moving forward with faltering steps and lack of faith can make things worse than before."

The Report examined the entire educational system except legal and medical education and claimed to provide some basic thinking and framework for taking at least the first step towards bringing about what may be called an educational revolution in the country. The Report pointed out that the most important and urgent reform needed in education was to transform it in such a way as to relate it to the life, needs and aspirations of the people and thereby to make it a powerful instrument of social, economic and cultural transformation necessary for the realisation of the national goals. To meet these goals, it further added that the educational system should be developed in such a way as to increase productivity, achieve social and national integration, accelerate the process of modernisation and cultivate social, moral and spiritual values. Within the context of these national objectives, the Report further elaborated in broad terms the main functions of the universities in the modern world as " (1) to seek and cultivate new knowledge, to engage vigorously and fearlessly in the pursuit of truth, and to interpret old knowledge and beliefs in the light of new needs and discoveries; (2) to provide the right kind of leadership in all walks of life, to identify gifted youth and help them develop their potential to the full by cultivating physical fitness, developing the powers of the mind and cultivating the right interests, attitudes, and moral and intellectual values; (3) to provide society with competent men and women trained in agriculture, arts, medicine, science, technology and various other professions, who will also be cultivated individuals imbued with a sense of social purpose; (4) to strive to promote equality and social justice and to reduce social and cultural differences through diffusion of education and; (5) to foster in the teachers and students, and through them in society generally, the attitude and values needed for developing the 'good life' in individuals and society."

In addition to stressing these broad functions which were believed to be somewhat universal with all universities any where, the Report emphasised that Indian Universities had to shoulder some special responsibilities in the present state of her social and educational development. The Report, therefore, highlighted the function that "First and foremost they must learn to strive to serve as the 'conscience of the nation', as assessors of the national way of life, and this responsibility becomes all the greater in the absence of an enlightened public opinion. So far, the Indian universities have not performed. this function adequately. This may be due either to apathy or failure to recognise the importance of this role or to the traditional belief that scholarship and academic excellence thrive only in isolation from the clamour of the multitude. To discharge this function properly, the university teachers should cultivate not only intellectual integrity, courage and scientific knowledge, but also win public confidence. Unless they have the high ambition to make an impact on the quality of social thinking and endeavour, they will not be able to help in moulding a new society which will not merely cherish high values, but actually provide opportunities for living them. Another special responsibility of the Indian universities is to develop programmes of adult education in a big way and to that end, evolve a wide-spread network of part-time and correspondence courses.

Above all, it will require that all universities function as agencies for a deep and careful study of local, regional, and national problems, to which Government, public and private organisations and industry may turn for advice and guidance. Yet another responsibility of the Indian universities in the present context is to strive to assist the schools in their attempts at qualitative self-improvement. For this purpose, universities should conduct experimental schools, run advanced courses for teachers in various school subjects, assume greater responsibility for the training of teachers at all levels, organise summer institutes for their in-service education, assist in the search for and development of talent, and develop new curricula, textbooks and teaching materials. Perhaps the most onerous responsibility which the Indian universities now have is to shake off the heavy load of their early tradition which gives a dominant place to examinations, to improve standards all around and by a symbiotic development of teaching and research to create at least a few centres which would be comparable to those of their types in any other part of the world."

The Report admitted that for the realisation of these objectives, our universities would need huge investments in terms of physical and monetary resources which were now beyond their reach.

It, however, advocated the need of a well-conceived and comprehensive plan for the development of higher education spread over the next twenty years, which should include three types of programmes: (1) a radical improvement in the quality and standards of higher education and research; (2) expansion of higher education to meet the manpower needs of national development and to some extent, the rising social ambitions and experiences of the people;, and (3) the improvement of university organisation and administration. The Report recommended the development of some major universities where first-class post-graduate work and research should become possible and in which academic standards would be comparable to the best institutions of their type in any part of the world.

In addition, it was recommended that at least one agricultural university should be established in each State. Some of the other recommendations included suggestions on the general improvement of the existing universities, development of affiliated colleges, improvement of teaching and evaluation, medium of education, student services, student unions, expansion of facilities, selective admission, college size, education of women, reorganisation of courses, study of social sciences, study of humanities, area studies, educational research, university autonomy, autonomy within a university, inter-university collaboration and role of the University Grants. Commission.

Since Independence, we have seen reports of many boards committees, commissions, panels and other groups. The Report of the Education Commission (1966) perhaps marked a turning point in the history of educational development. This Report clearly brought out that education could not be planned piece-meal, sector by sector, or scheme by scheme. The Report not only identified general and specific goals of education, but approached the subject comprehensively and recommended drastic reforms in the educational system necessitated by the changing social, economic and political conditions of the country. It also emphasised the necessity that the entire basis of education must be revolutionised to attune it properly to the national goals, needs and aspirations. How far the recommendations of the Report have actually been implemented is hard to say, but it seems to be clear now that the report did provide a sense of perspective, direction and a blue-print of the system of education to be ultimately evolved. Higher education has, more and more, been seen as a part of a wider process whose foundations need to be strengthened..

Moreover, the functions of the universities have been viewed in the larger context of the Indian society. As a matter of fact, soon after Independence, our respected leader, Nehru had also written somewhat on the same lines when he viewed that. "A university stands for humanism, for tolerance, for reason, for. progress, for the adventure of ideas and for the search for truth. It stands for the onward march of the human race towards even higher objectives. If the universities discharge their duty adequately, then it is well with the nation and the people. But if the temple of learning itself becomes a home of narrow bigotry and petty objectives, how then will the nation prosper or a people grow in stature ? A vast responsibility, therefore, rests on our universities and educational institutions, and those who guide their destinies. They have to keep their lights burning and must not stray from the right path even when passion convulses the multitude and blinds many amongst those whose duty it is to set an example to others. We are not going to reach our goal through crookedness or flirting with evil in the hope that it may lead to good. The right end can never be fully achieved through wrong means."

But it must be pointed out that there has been no dearth of documents and reports during the last three decades, which have not advocated the reorganisation of the total educational system, especially in the field of higher education, What has actually happened can be described as merely an expansion of the colonial system with a few marginal changes in the structure, content and techniques of education.

Goals in Enrolment

Higher education which is viewed essentially as post-secondary education, is imparted through Arts and Science colleges, professional institutions and universities. During the last thirty years there has been an increasing emphasis upon the expansion of facilities for higher education, especially in engineering and technology, medicine, agriculture and veterinary services. By 1975, the total number of universities are reported to have exceeded eighty with more than three thousand and five hundred colleges affiliated or attached to them. The enrolment is estimated to have gone beyond three million students, which is double the enrolment only a decade ago. It is now projected that this number will increase to five million by the end of the Fifth Plan and to ten million by the end of this century.

The fields of engineering, technology and medicine, which play a vital role in facilitating the processes of socio-cultural change, received somewhat special attention in the past fifteen years and were given substantial public funds. In 1951, there were 53 engineering and technical institutes at the degree level with an intake capacity of about 4, 800 students; and 89 institutions at the diploma level for about 6, 200 students. By 1970, the number of degree institutions rose to about 140 with an annual admission capacity of 25, 000 students, and to about 300 diploma institutes for 69, 000 students. In subsequent years, the intake capacity both for the degree, and diploma institutions was somewhat reduced in view of the incidence of periodic spells of unemployment among' engineering graduates. The Fourth Five Year Plan was forced to initiate a programme mainly based upon the recommendations of the University Commission which attempted to place a greater emphasis on the improvement of quality and standards in the engineering and technical institutes as compared to the expansion of physical facilities and increase in enrolment. Despite the greater potential needs of technical personnel in a society where rapid industrialisation is taking place, the fall utilisation of trained manpower has presented problems and dilemmas which are likely to receive more attention in the years ahead. In this context, it should be noted that the lack of employment opportunities within one's own country on the one hand and the introduction of somewhat liberal policies of immigration by some "Western countries on the other have brought forth a world-wide new phenomenon usually labelled as brain drain in the seventies. The full implications of this phenomenon have yet to be studied and worked out.

It is well known that India continues to have lowest standards of health for the bulk of her population as reflected through, high infant mortality rates, low per capita consumption of food and high morbidity rates for almost every type of physical and emotional maladjustment. However, it is gratifying to note that rapid strides have been made in the field of medical education. At the time of the First Five Year Plan, there were 30 medical colleges at the degree level and 4 colleges for the training of licentiates. By the end of the Fourth Plan, the number of medical colleges had increased to about 100, with an admission capacity of 12, 000 which was only 2, 500 in 1951. It is projected that the number of doctors will increase from an estimated 70, 000 in 1960-61 to 176, 000 in 1979. There has also been considerable expansion of facilities for the training of nurses, health personnel and other para-medical staff. In a country where there are tremendous problems of ill-health and high incidence of mortality, the need for all categories of medical personnel can hardly be overemphasised. Nevertheless, the plans, programmes and projects have often failed to utilise fully the services of trained medical and health personnel. It seems rather ironic that even medical graduates do not find adequate and suitable employment opportunities. There has been a considerable drift of medical personnel to other parts of the world, especially to the United States during the decade of 1965-75. It seems that the national government has been a helpless spectator to watch this continuous flow and took no effective measures to stop export of medical personnel.

In other fields such as agricultural and veterinary services also, there has been a rapid expansion of facilities in recent years. At the present time there are about 100 institutions with a capacity of 15, 000 students. The Draft Fifth Plan does not envisage any further expansion. The Plan stresses the need for the improvement of standard and quality of education, consolidation of post-graduate education, orientation of curricula and courses to suit the changing needs of agricultural development, strengthening of inter-institutional collaboration and development of centres of excellence. The enrolment in arts, commerce and sciences both in colleges and universities is reported to have increased by 0.2 million during each of the First and Second Plans, and by 0.5 million in the Third Plan. By the end of the Fifth Five Year Plan, about five million students are expected to be enrolled in our colleges and universities. According to the Plan the main problems which confront higher education are: its rapid expansion without a corresponding increase in physical facilities, lack of coordination with the social life of the community, widespread lowering of standards consequent on rapid expansion of the student body unaccompanied by concomitant expansion in the size and quality of the teaching community and increasing incidence of unemployment among university graduates.

The Draft Fifth Five Year Plan essentially reiterated goals put forward earlier in 1968, and reported that the main strategy for the development of university education will, therefore, have to be such as to ensure that, while the social demand for higher education, particularly for satisfying the rising expectations of the newly emerging socio-economic groups continues to be met, indiscriminate expansion of facilities is not allowed to further dilute the standards of university education. Most of the university courses will also need to be restructured so that the students completing their education are enabled to become productive members of society.

The Draft Plan also stressed the need to establish a closer link between education and employment on the one hand and between education and social environment on the other. The goals and policies adumbrated by the University Commission in 1968 have been generally repeated and highlighted. "What has been actually achieved is often left for our imagination. Of course, some steps have been taken to restrict the rapid expansion of higher education and to vocationalise high secondary education, enabling large numbers to enter employment at the end of the secondary stage. Further, it seems to have struck a new note by advocating (1) flexibility in curriculum selection; (2) introduction of vocational courses to increase employability of graduates; and (3) linking up of courses With practical problems and their social utilisation.

Spectre of Educated Unemployment

Ideally it is true that a society which has embarked upon the introduction of large-scale programmes of economic and social development requires an increasing expansion of facilities for higher education. Both the formulation of programmes and their implementation and administration call for a constant flow of trained personnel in almost every branch of knowledge. There is no doubt that the rapid pace of industrialisation during the past twenty-five years has been accompanied by significant changes in the occupational structure and has promoted new avenues of employment. But the absorption of formally educated persons into gainful employment has considerably lagged behind, with the result that thousands of graduates with university degrees and diplomas are unemployed at present. The reports of the Five Year Plans furnish us with a general picture of this problem. The relatively high incidence of unemployment among the educated clearly points out that there is an economic waste of scarce resources in educating and training young persona who then fail to get absorbed in the productive labour force. In recent years, a large number of highly educated persons is increasingly seeking emigration to the United States and other countries. The political implications of persistent unemployment seem to be disastrous for a society where the problem of lack of national integration and identification is already breeding discontent, distress, discord and dissension. Although it is fully recognised in governmental reports that the problem of unemployment among the educated is one of national importance and that it has serious social, economic and political consequences, the various solutions which have been either planned or implemented have failed to tackle the challenge of unemployment effectively.

It must be mentioned here that the problem of unemployment among the educated is a part of the wider problem of general unemployment. Further, it should also be added that this problem is constantly being accentuated partly by the rapid growth of population itself. Actually, the magnitude of the problem is known primarily in general terms and no precise data are available. For the study of urban unemployment, the reports of the National Sample Survey, by far, furnish the most extensive data; socio-economic surveys of selected cities form another source of information; and the reports of the Planning Commission, of the Directorate of Resettlement and Employment, Ministry of Labour, and of ad-hoc committees constitute another source of data. Despite the availability of such reports indicating grim statistical picture of the over-all unemployment throughout the country, they have often failed to bring to surface the misery and utter despair of those young persons who manage somehow to receive higher education but do not find worthwhile opportunities to eke out even their living, not to say of fuller opportunities for the use of their knowledge and talent. The magnitude and nature of the problem concerning unemployment are often overshadowed by the practice of the joint family system and the existence of other mutual aid arrangements of caste groups especially in villages and towns. The Report of the Study Groups on Educated Unemployment published in 1956 had provided an estimate of the number of educated unemployed at half a million persons. All available sources seem to indicate that the proportion of the educated unemployed has considerably risen in recent years. In Slay 1969, the National Labour Commission is reported to have recommended a crash programme to fight the problem of unemployment. Unfortunately no step has proved to be effective till today in the year 1978!

Culture and Education

The foreignness of higher education is so much all-inclusive that its very language in which higher education *is* imparted or acquired or expressed has been a foreign language. For this reason the higher education system has come to depend completely for its growth and development on the western culture and it still continues to derive an over-riding inspiration from it. Reviewing the vocation of the Indian intellectual, Shils has described this state of affairs vividly through somewhat in exaggerated terms, when he writes that, "in general, India has established a modern intellectual class, modern in its aspirations and in its intellectual procedures and substantive interests, but it has not yet developed an effective modern intellectual tradition which permeates the intelligentsia as a whole nor has it succeeded in generating effective intellectual traditions in the various fields of modern intellectual work. In the natural and the social sciences, in political writing and in literature, it is not yet impelled by its own genius. There are notable exceptions to this proposition in nearly every field; but in the main, the chief impression one gains from a survey of the output of the modern Indian intellectual class is a lack of ferment, a deficient vigor, an impoverishment of curiosity, a feebleness of the forward reach".

Nothing reveals more clearly the alien aura of higher education than the manner in which its curriculum is organised today. After tracing briefly the history of higher education, the report of the University Education Commission (1949) had pointed out unequivocally that our education must be Indian, *i.e.,* built on the foundations of our country's history and spirit, if it was to be true education and not just a superficial veneer of hastily applied and, therefore, easily scraped-off polish. The report had farther emphasised that the higher education must not only preserve and spread the treasures of the past but also add to them by research and discovery. Still more recently another Education Commission (1966) reported that the existing system of education was largely unrelated to Indian life and that there was a wide gulf between its content and purposes, and the concerns of national development. The report had also asserted that if higher education was to meet the purposes of a modernising democratic and socialistic society, what was needed was a revolution in education which in turn would set in motion the much desired social, economic and cultural revolution. In connection with the dominance of foreign influence on our higher education, the report observed that "the centre of gravity of Indian scientists working in fields which are internationally cultivated still tend to look outside India for judgment of their work, for intellectual models of the problems which they study, for the books they read, and for their forum of appreciation and approval". This state of affairs has been considered damaging by almost all committees, commissions and many individual scholars who have ever examined the system of higher education in the country.

In every society, education at all levels is highly influenced by its culture and the various dimensions connected therewith. What a society wants its children and young persons to learn and practise primarily -depends on the cultural values it holds. The functions of education, therefore, rest not only on the ideals visualised and formulated by the society for its future, which are usually reflected in the Constitution and legal structure and also upon the dominant mores of the society. Basically, sociologists regard education as a distinctively social phenomenon or a social institution, which like other social phenomena or social institutions, is a product of the culture itself. Durkheim indicated, long before the modern sociology of education arose, that education was something essentially social in character both in its origin and functions. He was emphatic in pointing out that differences in socio-cultural needs would play a major role in this type of educational programmes which would be established in various societies. In line with this thinking, the emergence and development of educational sociology in the United States, which began around the First World War and continued till the Second World War, led to the publication of extensive and significant literature on social foundations of the American educational system. Although American sociologists in recent years have preferred to call sociological analysis of education as sociology of education, yet the old theme of socio-cultural foundations of education continues to receive considerable attention emphasising the educational system as a social microcosm of the larger social system. The voluminous American literature which is available on the subject has, however, completely neglected the growth and development of educational systems in those countries of Asia and Africa which had been under the colonial rule of European powers for hundreds of years. In such countries the western culture flowed all these years and as a result of which the modern educational systems took their birth, super-imposing themselves the traditional patterns of education and life. As a matter of fact, the educational system in such countries especially higher education, has not become part of the self-reproduction process of the dominant institutional system and has been unable to free itself from its foreign origin and connections; rather it continues to derive its inspiration from the intellectual output which emanates from the culture and society of the West. It is unfortunate that Indian sociologists have undertaken little research on the different facets of their own educational system. For the first time, Indian scholars showed some interest in the sociology of education, when a Seminar was organised in December 1964.It is beyond doubt that Indian higher education in general is still dominated by foreign elements and there is an urgent need for "Indianisation". The need to develop Indian education at all levels, especially higher education on the cultural foundations of the Indian society is apparent. It is from the culture itself that education should be created if it has to become meaningful. Culture embraces philosophy, religion, science as well as folklore and superstitions; it includes moral beliefs, standards of good and evil and of right and wrong. As a matter of fact, every culture has its distinctive way of life and its indigenous pattern not only exists on the explicit level alone where it is consciously expressed, but on the implicit, half conscious, emotional and perhaps mythical level as well. Underlying this way of life, every culture has a set of dominant values which exercises tremendous influence on all aspects of life. Education, too, is immersed in such values because, it is always normative in character.

All societies must cope with the task of transmitting their cultural traditions to the new generation and, therefore, develop formal educational institutions at different levels. These institutions and hence education cannot become a social institution and an integral part of the culture, if there exists a wide divergence between the dominant religio-philosophical foundations and the basis of the educational system. In a society which is undergoing a rapid social change, education in general plays a vital role not only as a socialising process but as a major instrument to promote directed socio-cultural changes. In this context, higher education especially higher education in social sciences has to shoulder greater responsibilities of social statesmanship and to develop leadership, with commitment to social reform and social change. Social sciences relate to those fields of human knowledge which deal with group aspects of man's life and include the study of the processes and mechanisms of society itself; they are mostly concerned with those basic elements of culture which determine the general patterns of human behaviour. The humanities are closely related to social sciences, because both study man and his culture, and they are primarily concerned with man's attempt to express spiritual and aesthetic values through literature and arts and to discover the meaning of life through religion and philosophy, whereas social sciences are attempting to collect a vast amount of empirical data through scientific procedures so as to build general theories about the structure and functioning of different societies.

Several important issues have been left out from this discussion. Among those which have received considerable attention in recent years are: (1) financing of higher education, (2) governance of universities with reference to student's participation, (3) higher education and the backward classes; (4) the quality" of higher education and the system of examinations. Among the issues on which little work has been done so far are those relating to the student-teacher relationship and need for the cultural foundations of higher education.

REFERENCES

Annual Reports of the University Grants Commission.

Education in *India,* 1969-70 (New Delhi, 1976), and *University Development in India, Basic Pacts and Figures,* 1970-71 (New Delhi, 1974).

Edward Shils, *The Intellectual 'Between Tradition and Modernity: The Indian Situation* (The Hague, 1950), p. 24.

Emile Durkheim, *Education and Sociology,* translated by Sherwood Fox (New York, 1956).

M.S. Gore and Others, Papers in the *Sociology of Education in India*

(New Delhi, 1967) and by the same authors. *Field Studies in the Sociology of Education* (New Delhi, 1970).

R.K. Mookerjee, *Ancient Indian Education* (London, 1938) and R.C. Majumdar, et al., *History and Culture of Indian People* (Bombay, 1954).

T. N. Madan, *Doctors in Society* (Delhi, 1977).

T.N. Dhar, *Education and Employment in India* (Calcutta, 1977); C. Parvathamma, *Problems of Employment of University Graduates* (Bombay, 1977); and Total *Employment* (New Delhi, 1972).

Tara Chand, *Influence of Islam on Indian Culture.* (Allahabad, 1954).

5

Strains in American Social Work Education

It may be true that social work has emerged as a profession in the United States during the last three decades, with its own professional cadre, training programmes, professional ethics and professional organisations. But it is equally true that the vast majority of people who are known as social workers have little or no professional training, and that the public image of social work still remains hazy. Moreover, some remnants of the traditional social philosophies, popularly known as Social Darwinism and the Protestant Ethic, which have been dominant in American culture until recently, continue to retard the growth and development of comprehensive social welfare services, thereby undermining the progress of professional social work. The discovery of poverty pockets and the mounting racial tensions in the United States have also led to considerable pressures on the traditional social work approaches to social problems and professional training. The need for welfare at many levels and the development of social work education for all these levels also present a great challenge to the profession. The emergence of private practice in social work has further confronted the profession with the problem of reconciling the social ideology of social work and the profit-making practice of private social work.

Historically, American social work education, since the end of World War I, has been under the influence of Freudian psychology, which led to the development of courses on social casework and other related areas as the core of social work training. Moreover, the dominant values of private enterprise, individualism, materialism, and success on the one hand and the philosophical values of a Judeo-Christian heritage on the other, which underlie the culture of American society, have continually reinforced American social work philosophy, principles and techniques based upon psychological and psycho-analytical knowledge. The new demands on social work which began in the depression era, and the wider opportunities opened up for social workers by the social legislation of the fifties and sixties have certainly caused some of the American schools of social work to extend the scope of their teaching within the general framework of psychological orientation and social casework principles. In recent years, the Council of Social Work Education has shown considerable interest in exploring and developing a variety of approaches to the training of social workers at the undergraduate level, although the recommendations of the Curriculum Study in terms of a continuum of undergraduate-graduate education for social work were rejected by the Curriculum Committee of the Council itself.

Although courses have been better standardised, educational standards improved and the content of courses expanded since the establishment of the Council in 1952, the social work curriculum in general is still over-shadowed by the teaching of social casework and the psychological dimensions of human personality. The ability of the schools to prepare students for practice in highly individualised casework and probably in group work cannot be questioned. However, not more than a quarter of American schools of social work offer major courses in community organisation, and still fewer in such fields as social research, social administration and social policy. In fact, many of the schools which claim to offer a major sequence in community organisation are not even fully equipped in terms of suitably trained faculty and proper field placements. Consequently, the traditional conception of community organisation continues, with little emphasis on contributions from the fields of anthropology, sociology, economics and political science. The Curriculum Study revealed that different areas of social work practice and education have developed somewhat unevenly. Bisno even pointed out that much of the graduate curriculum is not of graduate calibre, since it necessarily has to "introduce" the student to many areas for which there is no foundation of specific pre-requisite knowledge on which to build. In its Curriculum study (1960), the Columbia University School of Social Work not only emphasised these gaps in social work education, but also the need to raise intellectual standards throughout the entire curriculum. As regards the international aspects of social work, few schools offer comparative courses on culture, welfare services, or systems of social security. The training and preparation of faculty members for teaching about international social welfare are woefully inadequate. Although several thousand foreigners have received their social work training in these schools during the last three decades, American social work educators admit that most of their schools do not have relevant course offerings and suitable teaching staff for training social workers from less developed countries. The existence of these gaps is recognised in professional articles and the proceedings of professional conferences, but few concrete steps have actually been taken to remedy these failings. The traditional pattern of education, dominated primarily by courses on social casework and social group work, continues to flourish, and even forms the basis of international cooperation in social work education, and is exported to other countries.

Cross-Cultural Diffusion of American Social Work Education

Since the end of World War II, the dissemination of American conceptions of social work education has influenced considerably the development of such education in the less developed countries, such as India in particular through expatriate American social workers and social work educators through American Embassies and Consulates where social welfare personnel were employed, through American social work study material, which was exported generously, and through American-trained people returning to their own countries. Some of the earlier schools of social work in India were actually established and developed by American social workers; they were often directed, and sometimes financed by Americans. Further, in 1956, the American Council on Social Work Education and the Ministry of Education of the Government of India agreed on a plan under which a number of American social work educators came to teach in Indian schools of social work, and many Indian scholars were sent as students to American schools of social work.

The diffusion of American social work education seems to have been based on the assumption that human beings everywhere have common human needs and human motivations on the one hand, and that principles, methods, and techniques are universally applicable on the other. This view is widely accepted in American social work, and is advocated through American-sponsored programme and international agencies. These are, however, untested assumptions. Actually, international studies completed by the United Nations and its allied agencies have increasingly recognised the heavy influence of social, cultural, economic, and political conditions on the practice of any form of social work, and have strongly advocated the development of indigenous teaching materials. The field of international social welfare still remains undeveloped theoretically or conceptually. It is high time that India should organise the much-needed research programmes to evaluate the applicability and effectiveness of American social work values, knowledge, skills, and methods to Indian conditions, and also to determine how far we can meaningfully adopt them in different fields of social welfare. At the other end, American social workers and social work educators must learn to accept the existence of cultural variability and the need for developing indigenous approaches to social work.

Organisation of Indian Social Work Education

Since the main inspiration for the establishment of formal training programme in India came from the United States, most of the schools of social work in India were initially created outside the traditional system of higher education. Moreover, as in America, graduate training was exclusively emphasised, with the result that little attention has yet been given to the organisation of social work education of the undergraduate level.

The first training institute was the Sir Dorabji Tata Graduate School of Social Work, established in Bombay in 1936. By 1970, training in social work at the graduate level had become available in thirty different institutions, both under the auspices of existing universities and of independent bodies, and almost all assisted in some way from American sources, in the form of technical knowhow, study material, or funds. A large number of social education centres, village level workers' training centres, agricultural institutes for rural welfare workers, and family planning training centres were also established, usually sponsored by the Central Government, but sometimes by voluntary organisations; these too offer courses on social work based on the pattern of American schools of social work.

Broadly speaking, as in the U.S.A., there are three components of social work education: social work curriculum offered in the classroom, field-work offered in a social agency, and research experience provided by a combination of the classroom and fieldwork agency. Within this general pattern, there is some diversity of emphasis partly determined by the availability of resources and facilities. The academic work is generally centred around courses dealing with (a) human growth and development, (b) social welfare services and social policies, (c) methods of social work, and (d) special areas of study. As in U.S.A., there has been a trend since 1960 to give less attention to the study of traditional social sciences, so that the coverage given to such themes as those of Indian culture, social structure, social institutions, and social change has been considerably reduced. At the same time, greater emphasis has been laid on courses on human growth and development, implying the over-riding importance of such methods as social case-work and social group-work on the one hand, and such specialties as family social work, medical social work, school social work and psychiatric social work on the other. The field-work ranges from weekly observations of work in different agencies to fifteen hours per week of regular work experience for two years; other practices include institutional visits, study tours, work camps and block field-work. The uneven patterns of field work have resulted in uneven standards of training, because there are few social welfare agencies in which the student can get appropriate work experience, and few qualified field work supervisors who can help him to integrate learning from experience. As regards the third component, almost every school of social work prescribes the completion of a research project based on some sort of field investigation of a social problem as one of the requirements for the Master's degree in social work. The topic selected is usually concerned with the student's area of interest or specialisation. Although the schools emphasise the individual research project of each student, some schools are experimenting with the idea of group research projects, a trend which is also emerging in the United States. Almost all schools offer at least one course on social research, which is believed to be of elementary level. As the teacher is so much burdened with a heavy teaching load and direct field-work supervision, he does not actively assist and guide the student in the selection of a suitable topic for research or in the design of his study. Consequently, it has been found that most of the research projects completed at the schools are on topics of little importance to Indian social work, and have failed to contribute any comprehensive knowledge based upon Indian life.

Indian Social Work Specialties

An analysis of the bulletins of the various schools of social work indicates that they offer training in such specialised fields as medical social work, family social work, psychiatric social work, institutional and correctional administration, rural welfare, tribal welfare, labour welfare, and community organisation. The growth of many of these areas has been largely influenced by the American pattern of social work education, having little regard to the prevailing social, cultural, economic and political conditions in Indian society. There are at present no well-defined categories of welfare personnel for which social work training is considered essential, except in the case of labour welfare. Medical social work is practised in not more than two dosen hospitals in the entire country, almost all located in the large metropolitan cities of Mumbai, Chennai, Kolkatta and Delhi. In a society where medical facilities and personnel are still grossly inadequate to meet some of the basic health needs, and where the incidence of morbidity is still very high, the development of medical social work as practised in the United States and other Western societies seems to be completely irrelevant. It is, therefore, not surprising that students specialising in medical social work often find employment in other related fields. It will be a long time before medical social work based on social casework techniques and therapeutic orientation will become widespread in our hospitals. Even in the United States, where medical social work is relatively well-developed, it is far from being widespread, and not every hospital in metropolitan cities has a separate department of medical social service.

Another specialisation offered by some schools of social work is psychiatric social work. In the United States and some other Western countries, this seems to be more widely practised, though it is not defined in precise terms. The first psychiatric social worker in India was employed in 1937 at the child guidance clinic of the Tata Institute, the first one of its kind in the country. During the next ten years, not more than three or four psychiatric social workers were ever employed, but in subsequent years there was a very slow but steady increase in employment for such workers in various settings. Problems of mental morbidity certainly do exist, though there are no reliable estimates; but it is well known that in the field of mental health our level of services is extremely poor. Provision for the treatment of people suffering from mental disorders and mental deficiency is not only inadequate, bat there are not enough institutions and workers to provide barely elementary forms of custodial care. In this context, the creation of a class of functionaries who will study the patient as a person in his social situation and analyse environmental factors does not seem to be justified. Our primary objective should be to strengthen and improve the existing institutions so as to provide better care and treatment to those patients who are severely affected by mental illness; we should give lowest priority to psychiatric social work, even if it is considered an important component of treatment according to Western standards of medical service. Indian, culture contains two potential assets for the protection and promotion of better mental health; the therapeutic value of Hindu religion and Hindu psychology, which is based upon several systems of yoga practices, and the use of indigenous medicines to relieve both physical and mental illness. The teaching of professional social work, however, fails to take these into consideration.

Family social work is yet another specialisation offered by many schools; in some cases, it is combined with child welfare. In the United States, family social work is fairly well-developed, and both public and private social welfare agencies offer family services. The main objective of family social work is to help the individual and members of his family to attain harmonious relationships so as to prevent individual and family disorganisation. This is achieved through the use of social casework, which includes marriage-counselling, family life education, and financial assistance. Although the leaders of American family social work claim that the family agencies provide services to all social classes, it will be fair to say that these agencies mainly serve people from low income groups. Many Indian social work educators and professional social workers who advocate the promotion of family social work seem to forget that the joint family is still the central institution in Indian society, and remains a great source of security and solidarity to its members. Perhaps the traditional family system has somewhat changed, both in its structure and function, as a result of increasing urbanisation, industrialisation, and modernisation, bat even today the joint family provides all the necessary services to its members and plays a vital role in an individual's life. Problems of marital conflict, disturbed parent-child relationships, fatherless families, unmarried mothers, single adults who are separated from their families, and the aged do exist in India, though little is known about their magnitude, as no reliable statistics are available. But, we do know that it is not so great, because they have neither weakened the existing structure and functioning of our family system, nor have they got any recognition in the Indian Five-Year Plans, which are aimed at achieving social and economic development of the country on a planned basis in the years ahead. Moreover, family welfare agencies, as known in the United States, do not yet exist in the country. Besides, the exponents of this approach do not seem to recognise the problems of teaching In the complete absence of study material on these subjects based upon Indian conditions and inevitably, in practice, they are driven to use American literature, concepts and methods derived from the fields of psychology, psychiatry, and psycho-analysis. This view has introduced unrealistic elements in training programmes for social work.

Indian schools of social work give considerable importance to academic courses on social group-work, and to field-work practice in group-work settings which are mainly recreational centres. Social group-work has come to be accepted in the U.S.A. as a basic method which uses group process and dynamics to help individuals improve their social functioning. This method is used by social workers with children, youth, adults, the aged, and with the physically or mentally unhealthy, to promote adjustment to different life situations through group experience. A large number of organisations offer group-work activities, and employment opportunities for social workers who are specialised in this method. Although most group-work is concerned with recreational and leisure-time activities, American social work claims to make certain distinctions in theory between social group-work and recreation, which are often difficult to maintain rigorously in practice because, social group-work tends to overlap with such other fields as adult education, physical education, and campaign, and a large number of social workers in group-work settings do not have professional training in social work even today. In India the field of leisure-time activities falls under the scope of adult or physical education, and Indian social work has failed to develop any collaborative arrangements with those concerned, so that there are few group-work agencies where social group-work is really practised. Accordingly, there are almost no employment opportunities for social group-workers in India, comparable to those in the U.S.A., where social group-workers are engaged in special organisations to render direct service to the members. Moreover, as specialisations in social work in India are still based on fields of practice rather than on methods of social work, as in the United States, the curriculum is unnecessarily over-burdened with courses in social group-work. Similarly, the field-work practice of students in recreational settings, which is usually supervised by instructors from physical education, provides little meaningful experience to Indian students.

Another specialisation which is often offered is institutional and correctional administration. The care of the destitute, the handicapped, the delinquent, and the criminal is mainly provided through institutions, both public and private. The ultimate goal of institutional care is said to be the prevention of social problems and the rehabilitation of people who become inmates of institutions. But if the existing level of social services is any indication, it is fair to say that even our institutional services are far from satisfactory, and experience chronic shortages of space, decent housing, proper equipment and qualified staff. The survey of social welfare agencies completed by the Central Welfare Board several years ago revealed that few Indian agencies had even a single professional social worker on their staff. Specifically in the field of correctional administration, the impact of professional social work seems to be insignificant. The level of services with regard to probation and parole, separation of juveniles from adult criminals, vocational training and after-care, and training of personnel for correctional administration is extremely low, even today. Even in the United States professional social work has not made much headway in correctional services, though case-work methods are frequently used in large institutions employing both professional and non-professional workers. The over-all shortage of trained personnel has become almost chronic. In some quarters, the place of social work in the field of correctional administration has even been questioned, and separate training institutions have been established in many states in the country.

As regards the specialisation designated labour welfare, historically this field has been included with social work because, industrial labour was looked upon as an underprivileged group for which special amenities and welfare services were provided through social legislation. Since the first school of social work was established in 1936, formal training for labour welfare has developed a close relationship with social work training programmes in the country. As this school was started by a trust financed by one of the largest industrial organisations in the country, training for labour welfare took root there. For a long time professional social work has been highly correlated with the field of labour welfare, not only by some of the schools themselves, but also by the employers, government officials, and leaders of voluntary social work. The emergence of the fields of personnel management and business administration on the one hand, the development of social insurance, trade unionism and social security measures, and increasing acceptance of welfare activities by the employer on the other, have confronted the schools of social work with a fundamental dilemma as to whether the new roles of industrial relations and personnel management belong to the field of social work.

The controversy about the training programmes for labour welfare as a part of social work education has received considerable attention in recent years, and the Tata Institute has now established a separate degree programme for personnel management and labour welfare, apart from the social work degree within its existing framework. The other schools are still hesitant to change the established pattern, or to abolish this field of specialisation from their training programme, because this specialisation is reported to be the only one for which social work training is statutorily recognised, for which major demand exists among applicants for admission to the schools of social work, and for which employment opportunities with better salaries are available. However, labour welfare also happens to be a field of study for which the schools are generally ill-equipped, because most of the faculty members do not have the requisite experience of working in industrial settings, the field-work consists mainly of observation, and courses of instruction are not necessarily consistent with the basic philosophy and methods of social work.

The other specialisations offered relate to the fields of rural welfare, tribal welfare, and urban community development; in one school at least, social research is provided as a specialised field of study. Almost 80% of the Indian population still lives in rural areas, where levels of living are very poor and large-scale programmes of rural development have been introduced throughout the country. Moreover, one-fifth of the population is classified as "backward classes", which include the 'scheduled castes and scheduled tribes; at the same time, one-fifth of the population lives in urban areas which need redevelopment. Although the schools of social work have offered courses on these subjects from the very beginning, and many schools claim to have such specialisations, it is well-known that Indian professional social work has failed to establish its role in rural tribal welfare and community development in general. The very fact that a large number of centres, institutes and orientation camps are training different categories of welfare personnel outside professional social work indicates the failure of the schools to assume responsibility for training such personnel. In recent years, some institutions training welfare personnel for the field of rural welfare have collaborated to some extent. However, even today no particular preference is given to social work graduates in these fields, nor have the schools reoriented their basic curriculum to the special needs and problems of Indian settings. In both rural and tribal welfare, social administration, community organisation and development, directed change and social research seem to be the most important areas for which social welfare personnel is needed; yet, it is in these very areas that the present social work training programmes are weak because of the over-riding influence of American social work education, where such fields are largely neglected even today.

Again, of the present time, one-fourth of the Indian population lives in cities with 100,000 and more inhabitants; both the number of such centres and the size of their population have increased in the last two decades. The need for specialised programmes of urban redevelopment and urban community development was accepted in the Fourth Five Year Plan; social welfare programmes are also being intensified, at least in large cities; family planning programmes are being introduced on a wider scale than ever before, and slum clearance and improvement programmes have been initiated to improve living conditions in Indian cities. It is true that all the schools of social work are offering courses on urban community development and organisation, but the Tata Institute of Social Sciences is the only one which has a well-established specialisation in this field. The Delhi Pilot Project established by the Delhi Municipal Corporation in 1959 to promote the growth of community life and to encourage the development of citizen participation in programmes of social welfare, has demonstrated that we need several categories of welfare personnel in the field of urban community development. Moreover, professional social workers have not yet established their specialised roles in this field on the basis of their competence. The Indian Council of Social Welfare has reported that very limited employment opportunities actually exist at present for social workers in the field of urban community development. In the context of Indian society, where the fields of health, education, and social welfare co-exist and often interpenetrate at a local level, community development, both in urban and rural areas, is essentially a multi-dimensional activity. Accordingly, any specialisation offered in community organisation needs to be established on an interdisciplinary basis which should take into consideration all the basic social sciences. The existing courses of training in community organisation at Indian schools rely heavily on American social work, and tend to neglect the contributions from economics, political science, sociology and cultural anthropology.

Indigenous Social Work Literature

Historically, the available indigenous literature covers broad subjects such as social problems, social structure, culture, social reforms, social education, community development and social planning, and is written primarily by social scientists. Some of this literature could be useful for training social workers in the context of Indian society. Such disciplines as social economics, social history, social anthropology, and rural sociology, and to a lesser extent political science and sociology, are fairly well established at many of the Indian universities where schools of social work function. The need and desirability for increasing collaboration between social work and other social sciences, as well as the humanities, seem to be greater today than ever before. In fact, social work often competes with other social sciences, and at times is even considered as a social science in India.

Many schools of social work are still known as institutes of social sciences, though their curricula are strictly based on American social work. It is rather unfortunate that the influence of psychology and psychiatry, as reflected through American social work literature, has taken root in the schools, and very little is offered on Indian philosophical and cultural values. All of these publications are compilations of contributions from various scholars from the fields of professional social work and sociology. Most of the authors have failed to consider the prevailing social, economic, and political conditions in India, or to provide any analysis of the applicability of Western conceptions of social work. Except for a few articles, scholarly discussion is frequently lacking, and little attempt is made to present a total picture of Indian conditions vis-a-vis professional social work.

Recently under the auspices of the Planning Commission, a monumental study, entitled Encyclopaedia of Social Work in India (New Delhi, Government of India, 1969) has been released. This consists of three volumes and seems to have been inspired by a similar publication issued in the United States by the National Association of American Social Workers. It includes a large number of articles about Indian social welfare services, history of social reforms, social legislation, social problems, social work methods, social work as a profession and other related subjects.

Although encyclopaedic in scope, the book seems to lack the scholarship which is usually associated with encyclopaedias. Some of the papers are sketchy or fragmentary; others are repetitions while, many give almost no picture of regional variation, and still others are entirely based upon foreign literature, of little relevance to the conditions prevailing in India.

Of course, a few articles are comprehensive in scope and scholarly in approach. Perhaps part three on social statistics; part four, the directory of social welfare agencies; and part five, the classified lists, will be of use to students of social welfare and to social administrators. The inclusion of the 'Code of Ethics' adopted by the National Association of the American Social Workers, the 'Social Work Curriculum Policy Statement' of the American Council on Social Work Education and 'Social Work Practice, a Working Definition', accepted by the National Association of American Social Workers, in this encyclopaedia demonstrates the overriding influence of American preoccupations and the absence of indigenous thinking in social work. Moreover, almost two-thirds of the contributors seem to have no formal education in any branch of social sciences or in social work.

Indian Social Work Periodicals

In the United States, a number of periodicals which propagate the growth and development of professional social work are published. In India, the *Indian Journal of Social Work* occupies a unique position in the profession of social work. The Faculty of Social Work, Baroda University, publishes irregularly a periodical entitled *Social Work,* carrying sketchy articles written mostly by students. The Central Social Welfare Board also publishes a popular periodical entitled *Social Welfare;* this has a wide circulation among voluntary social welfare services, but its articles are usually devoid of primary research data. After analysing the articles published in the *Indian Journal of Social Work* from 1957 to 1962, Khinduka and Anand reported that the picture of social work scholarship remains, on the whole, unsatisfactory, if not gloomy; but they consider the Journal broadly representative of the literature on social welfare and social work education in India. The *Social Work Forum,* founded in 1963, seems to have initiated a process of self-evaluation of Indian social work as a profession for the first time. A survey of the articles published between 1963-1970, however, reveals that most of them are, fragmentary, having little attraction for the serious student who wishes to find qualitative and quantitative data about the growth of social work as a profession in India on the one hand, and the application of Western conceptions to less developed countries on the other. However, even if the quality of the contributions in these periodicals may often be poor, their existence does provide opportunities for scholars to publish their findings or their views for wider circulation.

Culture and Social Work Education

In every society, education at all levels is highly influenced by its culture. What a society wants its children and young persons to learn and practise primarily depends on its cultural values. The functions of education, therefore, rest not only on the prevailing social, economic, and political conditions, but also on the ideals formulated by the society for its future, which are usually reflected in the Constitution and legal structure on the one hand, and in the dominant folkways of the society on the other. Basically, sociologists follow Durkheim in regarding education as a distinctively social phenomenon or institution, which is thus a product of the culture itself. The emergence and development of educational sociology in the United States, from the First to the Second "World "War, led to the publication of extensive and significant literature on the social foundations of the American educational system. Although American sociologists now prefer to call the sociological analysis of education the sociology of education, the socio-cultural foundations of education continue to receive considerable attention, emphasising the educational system as a social microcosm of the larger social system. The voluminous American literature on the subject has, however, completely neglected the growth and development of the educational systems in those countries of Asia and Africa which had been under the rule of European powers for hundreds of years. In such countries, so long exposed to Western culture, modern educational systems were superimposed on the traditional patterns of education and life, and have not yet become part of the self-reproductive process of the dominant institutional system, because they have been unable to free themselves from their foreign origin and nature; rather they continue to derive Its inspiration from the intellectual output emanating from the culture and society of the West. It is unfortunate that Indian sociologists have undertaken little research on their own educational system. For the first time, Indian scholars showed some interest in the sociology of education at a Seminar in December, 1964.

Indian higher education in general is still dominated by foreign elements, and the need for "Indianisation" exists. But social work education presents a unique case where foreign influence is almost universal, and there is a crying need for "Indianisation". Social work in any society is a product of its culture, and is highly influenced by the prevailing social, cultural, economic, and political conditions on the one hand, and by the ideals which the society has for its future on the other. The very basis of social work as a helping activity lies embedded in the culture. As we have seen, American social work relies heavily on the concept of personality, and therefore, on knowledge drawn from the fields of psychology and psychiatry. This frame-work continues to overshadow the role of socio-cultural factors, and even today, most of the voluntary social welfare agencies in the United States which offer professional social work are essentially social case-work agencies in practice. Although the need for a sociological frame of reference has increasingly been advocated in the United States in the last few years, what C. Wright Mills wrote almost thirty years ago seems to be still applicable to the large section of American social work which has, of late, claimed to have assumed the status of professional social work. Mills criticised the dominant emphasis in social work on situational aspects of social problems, and deplored its failure to see flaws in the social structure as contributing to pathological situations.

The four international surveys on training for social work published by the United Nations fully testify to that fact. Although these surveys have emphasised the need to develop a sociological perspective on social work, and have recognised the importance of knowledge about social, cultural, economic, governmental, and legal framework of the community in the social work curriculum, they also reflect considerable influence of the psychological frame of reference. Consequently, there seems to be an underlying belief in the practice-oriented social work education, as imparted in the United States, in most of the documents completed by the United Nations and its allied agencies. Moreover, these surveys, while admitting the variety of social philosophy in different countries, implicitly reveal a bias towards the social and political ideals which are held by American social work, even though they may not even be widely accepted in American society itself. The cultural context of social work has been regarded more as an article of faith, with meagre sociological analysis of the foundations and conceptions of social work in different societies. Again, these surveys have made little attempt to examine the applicability of American social work methods in other societies, accepting them as universal with little reservation. Most of the American social work literature itself is replete with a basic assumption that its philosophical tenets, methods, and skills are universally applicable.

No universal philosophy 'if social work has yet been presented, nor has it been demonstrated that any one model of social work education can meet the needs of societies with different religio-philosophical orientations. The setting or framework of the cultural complex of a society determines not only the conception of social work itself, but also its knowledge, skills, and methods also. Apart from the philosophical, social, economic, and political elements which dominate the cultural complex, social work is highly influenced by such factors as the type of welfare services available and the administrative structure of the organisations providing welfare services. In this connection the First United Nations Survey rightly observed: "There appears to be some measure of agreement that the social worker should have an understanding of *(a)* the cultural, political, social, economic forces affecting the lives of the people he serves and the social and economic problems that they face; *(b)* the legislation, services, and organisations created by the state and the community in order to promote social and economic well-being; (c) the patterns, both normal and abnormal, of the physical and psychological development of man; *(d)* the interaction of psychological and environmental factors in situations of cultural, social and economic stress; and (*e*) the purposes, principles and methods of social work.

The need to develop Indian social work education on the cultural foundations of Indian society, thus, becomes apparent. It is from the culture itself that education should be created if it is to become meaningful. Culture embraces philosophy, religion and science as well as folklore and superstition, and includes moral beliefs, standards of good and evil, and of right and wrong. In fact, every culture has its distinctive "way of life" or value system, which reflects the indigenous pattern not only explicitly, but also on the implicit, half-conscious, emotional and perhaps mythical level. Education is immersed in such values, because it is always normative in character. All societies must transmit their cultural traditions to the new generation, and must, therefore, develop formal educational institutions at different levels. These institutions, and the education provided cannot be an integral part of the culture if their values diverge markedly from the dominant religio-philosophical foundations. In a society which is undergoing rapid social change, education in general plays a vital role, not only as a socialising process, but also as a dominant instrument to promote directed socio-cultural changes. In this context higher education, especially in social work, has to shoulder responsibilities of social statesmanship and to develop leadership, with commitment to social reform and social change. Social work education which maintains the traditional conceptions of working with individuals, groups and communities, and which is primarily orientated towards facilitating and strengthening the individual's capacity to cope with his problems, seems to have little relevance to Indian society and culture.

Need for Indigenous Thought

We have seen that American study material is still widely used, and Indian social work educators have developed very little indigenous teaching material. Some attempts have recently been made by the schools of social work in Delhi and Baroda, but these sporadic efforts hardly affect the paucity of material based upon Indian conditions. In this connection the contribution made by the United Nations and its allied agencies should be noted. At the initiative of the Economic Commission for Asia and for the Far East, a working group on the development of indigenous teaching material was set up, which reported in 1964. The Commission also sponsored a training centre in September 1966, to offer to some social work teachers selected by their governments, an opportunity to make a systematic study of educational processes, to establish the main principles of curriculum-building, to clarify the impact of cultural factors on social work practice and education, to help select indigene as case records for teaching purposes in Asia, and to produce a workbook on social work education in some of the Asian countries.However, a cursory perusal of the reports and other material produced by the Commission reflects nothing but complete acceptance of American social work philosophy, methods, and skills. The Commission has assumed in most of its reports that "the fundamental principles and methods of social work may be universally applicable". Moreover, the organisation, administration, and writing of the reports of the Commission has usually been undertaken by social work teachers who have either been trained in American social work or have been completely identified with it for a long time. The Commission is directly connected with the United Nations Department of Economic and Social Affairs, whose activities and programmes have been mainly influenced, or controlled by American social work educators or scholars from other disciplines, so that the basic pattern of American social work education and social welfare programmes has been advocated for the use of less developed countries, implicitly or explicitly. There has been some re-thinking in the United Nations recently with regard to programme of social development and social work education. Pusic's report opened up a new perspective on the future development of social welfare programmes, including utilisation of social welfare experts, and the award of fellowships and training for social welfare personnel.

Earlier, at the Conference on International Social Welfare Manpower (1964), the United Nations delegate admitted that the reappraisal of the U.N. social welfare programmes had raised some doubts about the adequacy and suitability of their current approaches to the training of social welfare personnel for developing societies, and the usefulness of social work experts from industrially advanced nations to these societies. In September 1968, at the International Conference of Ministers responsible for Social Welfare organised by the United Nations, new perspectives for social welfare programmes were explored, and problems concerning training of social welfare personnel were also discussed. The report emphasises the need to develop new patterns of social work education and utilisation of social welfare and manpower. The sooner some concrete steps are taken to promote the goal of 'Indianisation' of professional social work, the better it will be, so that it can be relevant to the conditions in Indian society Indigenous study material is urgently required, and above all the need to develop a social administrative perspective on social work education is increasingly apparent.

6

Women Development Through Government Action

The Indian Constitution guaranted equal rights for men and women, but women did not get an equal share of attention or expenditures in government development programmes which adopted a welfare orientation toward women's issues. Since welfare expenditures were seen as non-productive, women's programmes were a low priority item in government budgets. In 1971 the Government of India appointed a committee to examine the status of women in order to aid in the policy-making process. Published in 1975, the report of the Committee on the Status of Women in India (CSWI), *Towards Equality*, documented that women were excluded from a large number of wage earning activities and that their employment situation was worsening as a by-product of the expansion of capitalism in India.

In the rural areas there had been an increase in indebtedness and in the number of agricultural labourers. Women's employment in manufacturing and mining had declined. *Towards Equality* drew attention to the large number of women working in the unorganised or IS about which few studies at that time existed.

During 1975 interdepartmental consultations were held by the Department of Social Welfare on strategies to improve the status of women. These consultations drew on the recommendations of the CSWI and the World Plan of Action adopted at the U.N. International Women's Year Conference at Mexico City. The Institute of Applied Manpower Research drafted a *National Plan of Action for Women (NPAW)* based on these consultations, and the *NPAW* was approved by Prime Minister Indira Gandhi and published by the Department of Social Welfare in 1977. A comparison of *Towards Equality* and *NPAW* shows the extent to which the perspectives of the policy makers were affected by the CSWI. In identifying the sources of women's oppression, *NPAW* (1977:12) directly quotes CSWI, "The impact of the transition to a modern economy has resulted in the exclusion of an increasing number of women from active participation in the productive process."

In the area of employment, *NPAW* acknowledged its reliance on *Towards Equality*. Many CSWI recommendations were included: e.g. extending the coverage of the Maternity Benefits Act, providing more creches, paying equal wages to men and women, and setting up a Women's Cell in the Ministry of Labour. The *NPAW* did not, however, accept the CSWI call for a women's quota in industrial training programmes or a provision for women to re-enter government after a five year leave to raise a family.

Indira Gandhi accepted the *NPAW* recommendations, but the implementation of the recommendations did not proceed smoothly. Government action on women's issues during the Emergency and the subsequent Janata Government was more appearance than reality. Nevertheless, women's economic issues had gained some government visibility by the 1980s. Since the submission of *Towards Equality,* one section of the women's movement has sought to shape national policy on women through elite political channels. For example, women's organisations in 1980 successfully pressurised the Planning Commission to include a chapter on women and development in the Sixth Five Year Plan.

In the summer of 1988 the economic problems of IS women received some national attention. Two important government sponsored reports, the draft *National Perspective Plan for Women 1988-2000 A.D.* and *Shram Shakti, the Report of the National Commission on Self-Employed Women* were being circulated in New Delhi.

The Department of Women and Child Development of the Ministry of Human Resource Development appointed the National Commission on Self-Employed Women, chaired by Ela Bhatt, on January, 5, 1987 and charged it with the task of conducting a comprehensive study of self-employed women workers and of suggesting measures to "remove constraints adversely affecting the interest of self-employed women." The National Commission decided to enalarge its scope of reference to include all women workers in the unorganised sector, and the government accepted this change. *Sharm Shakti* was signed in June 1988 and presented to the government in early July.

Also in January 1987 the Department of Women and Child Development set up a core group chaired by Margaret Alva, Minister of State, to assist in drawing up the *National Perspective Plan for Women 1988-2000 A.D. (NPPW),* prepared by the Women's Division of the National Institute for Public Cooperation and Child Development. The draft *NPPW* was signed on February 20, 1988, and was discussed at the first meeting of the National Advisory Committee on women, chaired by the Prime Minister on May 17,1988.

The draft *NPPW* was circulated during the summer, and a revised version was issued on October 10.

Although the *NPPW* has a broader focus than *Shram Shakti,* they each implictly embody a distinctive approach towards the state's role in women's economic development: a technocratic institutional approach in the *NPPW* and an organisational-facilitator approach in *Shram Shakti.* The *NPPW* reviews the approaches taken toward women in the Five Year Plans and government women's programmes and the situation of women in various sectors such as rural development, employment and legislation, and it suggests "interlinked and coverging strategies toward a holistic development of women by 2000 A.D." Its recommendations include strengthening existing policies and setting up two types of institutions to coordinate women's economic programmes: Women's Development Corporations at the central and state levels and a National Training Institute for Women. It endorses a technically improved version of the existing top-down approach to women's development with new women-specific institutions to ensure women get their share of services. For example, the *NPPW* suggests that the Women's Development Corporations would play a major role in supplying women with credit.

Shram Shakti contains chapters that provide occupational profiles and labour force analyses of women IS workers, examine the impact of macro policies on unprotected women's labour, and discuss factors that impede and facilitate organising IS women. Its recommendations include expansion of existing labour legislation to cover various groups of IS workers and the creation of new procedures, offices and bodies to facilitate oranisations of women workers bringing complaints about wages and working conditions to the government. For example, the report calls for separate labour commissioners for unorganised workers in each state, women's organisations and trade unions being vested with the right to bring complaints to labour court and the establishment of an Equal Opportunities Commission in the Central Government to investigate charges of discrimination.

A certain amount of controversy surrounded these reports. Jaya Arunachalam, a member of the National Commission, attached a note of dissent to the report, criticising its quality and stating that most of the information in the report had already been covered by the draft *NPPW*. In turn several articles in the press criticised the politics of the *NPPW*'s preparation and recommendations from a perspective sympathetic to the National Commission on Self-Employed Women *(Times of India* 6/28/88; *Hindustan Times* 7.8.88; Rai 1988; Sharma, 1988).

What do these controversies mean? First, the mere existence of the reports reflects the acquisition by IS women of a degree of what Nirmala Banarjee (n.d.) calls "political visibility": "Government support is not necessarily based on worker bargaining strength, specific skills or the justice of claims, but....[on] how far support to the group reflects favourably on the party's image." What facilitated the government making this connection were the successful organising efforts of groups such as the Self-Employed Women's Association (SEWA) of Ahmedabad led by Ela Bhatt and the Working Women's Forum of Madras led by Jaya Arunachalam (Sebstad, 1982; Chen, 1983; Neponen 1987; Azad, 1986). In recognition of her accomplishments, Ela Bhatt was nominated by the President of India to the Rajya Sabha and later appointed to the Planning Commission.

The acquisition of even a limited degree of political visibility creates a relationship between IS women workers and the government. The government can use this relationship to co-opt the IS women's organisations, but the organisations' leaders can also use this relationship to influence the government. The controversies surrounding the *NPPW* and *Shram Shakti* represent contending approaches concerning the state and IS women, and they represent competition for power to shape the government's agenda in this area.

While these reports demonstrate that women's issues have attained visibility, they do not guarantee that new laws to regulate women's employment or new policies to assist self-employed women will be enacted. Like the enquiries established to study the problems of sweepers and domestic workers discussed later in this chapter, these reports are only a potential first step toward policy-making. To what extent are women IS workers affected by existing labour laws? To what extent are self-employed women in the IS assisted by existing government development policies? It is to these questions that we turn in the remainder of the chapter.

Labour Legislation

In this section we outline some of the major legislation which could have some relevance to IS activities, noting judgments where the definitions have been changed or expanded. It is quite confusing to understand the variety of laws which apply to workers, since many different laws apply, and many of the major definitions have been subject to much litigation expanding or changing the definitions. Enforcement is a central problem as *Shram Shakti* (1988:99) points out:

Factories Act 1948 Labour legislation in India developed during the colonial period. The first law, passed in 1881, sought to control the hours of work of children in the textile factories. Later laws covered women and finally all workers in factories. The passage of such legislation served to demarcate a formal from as IS of employment. The use of labour legislation has been of limited use to these who are in the IS. The first problem is the definition of factory, the site of work. The second is the nature of the employer-employee relationship.

The Factories Act, which deals with working hours, leave, health and safety conditions was enacted to regulate the conditions of work of only those who were working in a "factory," defined as that having a fixed percinct in which "manufacturing" work was being carried out. The Factories Act as it presently stands applies only to those units in which either 20 or more persons are working without the aid of power or where 10 or more persons are working with the aid of power. The act, therefore, excludes from its purview a vast majority of workers who either work in their homes or in units which do not strictly fall within the definition of a "factory."

One consequence of the enactment of the Factories Act was that the employers in some industries found ingenious ways to avoid the applicability of the act to their units, by dividing their establishments into smaller units and giving workers work to do in their homes. In the best knows cases large *bidi* factories were shut down, and employers started issuing raw materials to workers who rolled the *bidis* at home and brought the final product to contractors. Since the workers were no longer applied to them.

Another obstacle in making the act applicable to all workers is the definition of worker:

> a person (employed directly or by or through any agency, including a contractor), with or without the knowledge of the principal employer, whether

for remuneration or not) in any manufacturing process or in cleaning any part of the machinery or premises used for a manufacturing process or in any kind of work connected with the manufacturing process or the subject of the manufacturing process.

The provisions of the Factories Act were applied for the first time to home-based workers in State *v* Alisaheb Kashim Damboli (1954 8 FJR 494) and Ramchandra Prasad *v* State of Bihar (1956 11 FJR 96). In Modern Match Industries Ltd. (1956 ILLJ 335) persons were required to report for work everyday and were given a particular quantity of raw material to work on at their homes. They were required to finish the work at their homes within a stipulated period for which they were paid at a fixed rate at the end of each month. It was held that the persons were employed for hire, and as the employer exercised sufficient control over them, they must be held to be workers under the definition of the act.

However, before the Supreme Court, in Chintaman Rao *v* State of M.P. (1958, 14 FJR 103), a restricted interpretation was put on the definition of the term "worker" in section 2 (b) of the Factories Act. A person would not be considered an employee of another person without a master and servant relationship between the two. The question of whether a relationship of master and servant exists between an employee and employer has been the subject of judicial consideration in a number of cases such as Dharanpradha Chemical Works Ltd. *v* State of Maharashtra (1957 ILLJ 477), Birdichand Sharma *v* First Civil Judge, Nagpur (1961 AIR SC 644), and D.C. Dewan Mohideen Sahib and Sons and Anr. and United Bidi Worker's Union Salem (1964 2LLJ 633). The meaning of the above judgments is that as long as there is supervision or control over the details of the work, there is a relationship of master and servant. Since this constitutes a contract of employment between the two, the provision of the Factories Act would apply to them. Thus it is not necessary that the worker works on the premises of the employer. Even if they were home workers as long as there was supervision and control over the work, the Factories Act could apply.

The landmark decision, Bhikusa Yamasa Kshatriya Pvt. Ltd. (1963 24 FJR 429), broadened the applicability of the Factories Act, stating that under section 85, power had been given to the state government under the act to decide with reference to local conditions whether it was desirable that the act should be made applicable to any establishment which was not covered by the definition of "factory' or to workers in a factory who were not entitled to the benefits of the act because of the definition of "employment." The difficulty, however, lay in the fact that the extension of the act was dependent on the notification being issued by the state government. The judgments after the 1960s broadened the interpretation of the definition of "worker." These cases were, however, primarily decided under the Industrial Disputes Act.

The enforcement authority under the Factories Act is the Chief Inspector and other inspectors appointed under the act who have the power to issue order to the factory owners. Any offenses under the Factories Act can be tried by the Magistrate's Court but only with the prior sanction of the factory inspector. Workers covered under the act can lodge a complaint with the factory inspector, but in the majority of such cases the factory inspector does not investigate or the employer is informed. A recent amendment to the act prohibits the factory inspector from disclosing any information given to him by the employee.

Shops and Establishments Act (1948): Those units which are not covered by the Factories Act are covered by state laws regulating the operation of shops and establishments. The Bombay Shops and Establishment Act, 1948, applies in Maharashtra. The short title to the act states that it is an act to consolidate and amend the law relating to the regulation of condition of work and employment in shops, commercial establishments, residential hotels, restaurants, eating houses, theatres and other places of public amusement or entertainment and other establishments.

The term "other establishments" is a comprehensive term and includes such other establishment as the state government may add by notification in the official gazette and declare to be an establishment for the purpose of the act. Certain guidelines have been set as to what constitutes an "establishment," and they are as follows:

It must carry out business, trade or profession in an organised systematic and commercial manner. The intention to make profit is not an essential part of the legal definition of trade or business. The activity must systematically and habitually be undertaken for production or distribution of goods or for rendering material services to the community. There must be co-operation between employer and employee. It is not necessary that there should be a fixed place or abode, premises or location from where business is carried out.

Under the act, a complaint can be lodged only by an inspector and with the previous sanction of an official such as the District Magistrate or the Deputy Commissioner of Labour. An amendment has been made to the act to allow an aggrieved person or a representative of a registered union to make a complaint without obtaining the sanction of the relevant authorities.

Industrial Dispute Act (1947): While the Factories Act deals mainly with terms and conditions of service, the Industrial Disputes Act (1947) was enacted to provide for the investigation and settlement of workplace disputes. The two most litigated definitions under the act are "industry" and "workman". Because the definitions are vague, there are conflicting judgments as to whether IS workers are covered under the act.

The wide scope of the definition of industry under the act has been the subject-matter of a number of judicial decisions, such as B.M. Bannerjee *v* P.R. Mukherjee (1953 1LLJ 195), Baroda Borough Municipality *v* Its Workmen (1957 1 LLJ 8), Corporation of City of Nagpur *v* Its Employees (1960 ILLJ 523), State of Bombay *v* Hospital Mazdoor Sabha (1960 ILLJ 251), Cricket Club of India *v* Bombay Labour Union (1969 ILLJ 77), Bombay Panj Rapole *v* Its Workman (1971 ILLJ 393). The confusion created by these decisions was resolved in the Bangalore Water Supply Case. The Bangalore Water Supply and Sewerage Board *v* A. Rajappa and Ors (1978 LIC S.C.) set out the dominant test criterion in order to determine what is an industry. These tests are : systematic activity organised by co-operation between employer and employee, and the production or distribution of material goods and services for the community. After the Bangalore Water Supply and Sewerage Board case, "industry" was broadly defined to include shops, hospitals, cooperative societies, professional offices, doctors, and lawyers. Thus a large number of workers who were not originally protected under the act were covered.

In a number of cases, including the Bangalore Water Supply case, domestic work was specifically excluded from the definition of industry. The reasoning given in the Bangalore Water Supply case was as follows:

> Domestic employment cannot be regarded as an "industry" because the employment of a domestic servant has no resemblance to trade, business or industry. Domestic servants have a calling or occupation but it cannot be said that their employment is an industry. Nor are the private householders employers who carry on an industry as contemplated by the Act. Further, there is no cooperation between capital and labour which is necessary to constitute the industry. The domestic servant renders services purely of a personal nature.

By a similar judicial reasoning home-based workers and other IS workers would equally be excluded.

Though the Factories Act recongises a worker who may not be directly employed by the principal employer, the definition of "workman' under the Industrial Disputes Act is much narrower. A workman under this act, includes any person employed in industry to do any manual unskilled or skilled, technical, operational, clerical or supervisory work. Thus, unlike the Factories Act it was not clear by a reading of the definition whether a workman engaged through a contractor in connection with the work of the "industry" would also be considered a "workman." It was therefore left to the courts to interpret the definition of workman according to the facts and circumstances of each particular case.

The test that stood out was the right of the master to control the servant not only in what he did but also as to the manner in which he did his work. In Shivnanda Sharma *v* Punjab National Bank (1955 ILLJ 688) the question was whether the dismissed worker was an employee of the bank or of the "contract treasures." It was held that the direction and control of the worker was completely vested in the bank. If a master employs a number of persons to do a particular job, the employees thus appointed by the servants would be equally servants of the master. The case concluded that it was not correct to say that persons appointed and dismissed by an independent contractor can in no circumstances be the employees of the principal party.

Similar principles were set out in Kanpur Mill Mazdoor Union and Muir Mills Co. Ltd. (1955 2LLJ 537) on who can be considered a "deemed" employee. Though the employees in the case were recruited through a contractor, the details of their work were supervised by the mill and so they were considered employees of the mill. The decisive test was whether the management had some measure of control over and could regulate the action of the employee during the time he was engaged in doing the work. In K. Keshav Reddiar and his workers (1956 ILLJ 139) goldsmiths were employed by the gold merchant to prepare jewels as per specifications and within a fixed time. They were paid according to the number of jewels prepared by them. Control over the work of such goldsmiths was retained by the person employing them. Hence, they were considered his workmen under the Industrial Disputes Act.

After the 1960s the courts broadened the definition of workman and held that the test of control was not in itself decisive, and other tests for determining the relationship of employer-employee were equally important particularly aspects relating to (1) ownership of tools (2) chances of profit (3) risk of loss.

Under the Industrial Disputes Act, complaints can be raised by the workman under the act in respect to dismissal, discharge, retrenchment, lay off, change in service conditions and lock outs or closures. However, these complaints cannot be directly raised before the courts. A complaint has to be first raised before the Government Labour Officer. Both the employer and employee are then called by the officer for discussions which can drag on for months. The Government Labour Officer has no power to ensure that the parties appear for the discussions. If negotiations fail, the complaint is then referred to a Conciliation Officer. In a majority of cases no settlement takes place. Then the Conciliation Officer submits a failure report to a government official who refers the matter to the relevant court. Once remanded to a labour court or industrial tribunal, a case can take upto four years or more. There is no scope for interim relief.

Contract Labour (Regulation and Abolition) Act, 1970: The objective of this act is to regulate employment of contract labour in certain establishments and to provide for its abolition in certain circumstances. It applies to every establishment in which 20 or more workmen are employed or were employed on any day of the preceding twelve months as contract labour and to every contractor who employs or employed 20 or more workmen under those conditions. This act could also to establishments or contractors employing less than 20 workers if the appropriate government issued a notification in the official gazette in this regard.

The provisions of this act do not apply to establishments in which work of only an intermittent or casual nature is performed. Discretion vests with the appropriate government to decide in consultation with the Central or State Board as to whether the work in question is of intermittent or casual nature. A contract worker is defined as one who is employed in or in connection with such work by or through a contractor with or without the knowledge of the principal employer. A contractor refers to a person who undertakes to produce a given result for the establishment other than a mere supply of goods to the establishment through contract labour or who supplies contract labour and includes a sub-contractor.

The procedure for prohibiting contract labour in a particular establishment is complex and lengthy. A complaint must be made to the Commissioner of Labour who investigates whether contract labour engaged in the establishment should be prohibited. The guidelines used include (1) work carried out must be integral to the work of the industry, (2) work should be of a perennial nature, (3) work is ordinarily done by regular workmen working in the establishment, and (4) the establishment should be able to absorb full-time workers. Even if the commissioner decides that contract labour must be abolished, he cannot pass an order to that effect. The power to prohibit the employment of contract labour in any establishment lies solely with the appropriate government.

The relevance of formal sector labour legislation to the IS: To what extent can IS workers make use of these laws for the improvement of their working conditions? Despite the positive interpretation given by the courts to the definition of the employer-employee relationship, home-based workers and contract workers have still not been able to enjoy the benefits of these acts. Judges are reluctant to touch the gray areas which would according to them open the flood gates to litigation if IS workers were to be covered by the various labour laws. In majority of cases of home-based work the employers normally operate behind the scene. The intermediaries or contractors play the dominant role. They directly employ the workers, the raw materials are furnished by them, and the work of the workers are supervised and/or controlled by them. The principal employer may never appear in the picture. Thus all or any one of the tests as propounded by the court may not apply to home-based workers.

The jobs undertaken by the contractor from the principal employer are viewed as contracts of service, i.e. the employer gives the entire job to the contractor whose job it is to complete the work. An overall specification is given but the manner in which it is to be done has ultimately to be decided by the contractor. The workers engaged to do the work are thus not considered to be employees of the principal employers. The employer is able to escape the provisions of the law by engaging a number of contractors. A case in point is when a large public sector company engages a large number of contractors to do the jobs of stitching the napkins. The work is not done at the site, and the raw materials are not given by the public sector undertaking. The contractors are required to perform a particular jobs i.e. stitch a number of napkins in a specified manner. The contractors then give out the jobs to a number of workers who stitch the napkins at home. The raw materials are given by the contractors; it is they who supervise the work and pay the workers. Under these conditions (which are common in income generation projects run by charitable groups) labour laws do not apply.

In the case of domestic workers, the work is looked upon as privatised. The home is not considered a factory, shop or establishment. The home owner is not considered to be a business owner. The work does not involve profit or loss. No commodities are produced. Hence the work of a domestic worker is looked upon as performing a "personal service." The home owner is entitled to pay any wage and no labour laws apply. The result is that working hours and payment of salary are totally arbitrary. There is no security of tenure and no terminal or retirement benefits.

Home-based workers can make use of the Industrial Disputes Act only if it can be shown that they are employees and that the place where they work is an "industry." In the case of domestic workers they are not considered as employees and the place that they work is not an "industry" as defined under the Industrial Disputes Act. In the case of private sweepers, only those working in a co-op. housing society are regarded as employees and then only if this society is considered as an "industry."

The majority of workers in India are outside the scope of most labour laws. The Government of India and state governments sought to improve the conditions of certain workers not covered by the laws discussed above by drafting specific acts including (1) Minimum Wages Act, (2) Bidi Workers Act and (3) Security Guards Scheme. We will briefly review these laws to see whether they could be extended to the groups under study or serve as a model for legislation for these groups.

The Minimum Wages Act, 1948: The Indian Parliament began to set minimum wages for low wage unorganised occupations in 1948. A list of trades for which the law would apply was drawn up in a schedule attached to the act. This schedule was not exhaustive, and governmental units were empowered to add occupations after providing notification. The Minimum Wages Act intended to ensure regular payment of minimum rates of wages without unauthorised deductions to vulnerable employees so that they would be able to make both ends meet. However, despite the policy of the legislature to include in the schedule those industries in which labour is being engaged on extremely low wages, a large number of unorganised labour are still not covered by the act. None of the occupations studied are covered. Furthermore the implementation of this act has been extremely ineffective.

Bidi and Cigar Workers (Conditions of Employment) Act 1966: Another way in which the government has attempted to regulate IS employment is through enacting legislation for a specific occupation as in the case of the Bidi and Cigar Workers Act. This act redefined employer, employee, and site of production to cover the millions of *bidi* workers in India. As a result of wide scale exploitation of the workers a number of committees were constituted to go into the working conditions of *bidi* workers. Legislation was passed in several states, but the industry was highly mobile and moved to areas where regulations did not apply. To prevent this practice, a central law was passed in 1966. Employers challenged the law in the courts, but it was finally upheld in the Supreme Court in 1974.

The Bidi Act contains provisions providing for the regulation of the contract system of work, licensing of *bidis,* definition of industrial premises, and matters pertaining to health, hours of work, rest periods, overtime, and annual paid leave. After the enactment of the Factories Act, the large *bidi* factories split up into smaller units to evade this law. A similar situation arose after the enactment of the Bidi Act in 1966: the employers switched to home-based workers. Although the act specifically extends to home-based workers, the enforcement has not been satisfactory.

Employers have found ways to circumvent the extremely wide definitions of employer-employee in the act. Employers began to introduce intermediaries who were neither contractors not sub-contractors. The employers sold the intermediaries the raw materials and bought back the finished product. The *bidi* workers were made to buy all the raw materials from the intermediaries and then sell them the finished product. In this situation it was argued that a market transaction was involved and there was no question of an employer-employee relationship. Despite all the problems, the Bidi Act is one of the only examples where the state has tried to develop legislation on behalf of home-based workers. After the enactment of the Bidi Act, the test of control underwent drastic changes and was more broadly interpreted. It might be possible to amend this law to include other types of home-based workers.

The Private Security Guards Board Scheme: Yet another way in which the government has sought to regulate IS employment is through the creation of boards which set up tripartite committees that consist of representatives from labour, employers and the state and that arbitrate disputes for that industry. Boards have been created for security guards, dock labour, and *mathadi* (head loader) workers. As a case study we will briefly describe the Security Guards Act.

The Private Security Guards (Regulation of Employment and Welfare) scheme came into existence in 1981. It is applicable to the State of Maharashtra. Before the act, about 250 agents and agencies were operating in Greater Mumbai and Thane Districts, regularly supplying persons to work as security guards to various establishments. The object of the legislation was to eliminate the middle men and to create a pool of security guards and to supply them to the establishments through a board constituted for that purpose. The Security Guards Act includes provisions extending the Workman's Compensation Act and the Payment of Wages Act to these workers.

However, under the act direct access to the courts for redress of grievances in forbidden. The act provides for an internal grievance procedure requiring the Chairman of the Board to hear the concerned parties. These administrative intermediaries normally pass orders in favour of the Board and the employer. Further, if services of a security guard are terminated, there are no immediate remedies. There have been many allegations of nepotism and corruption within the board. Those who are favoured are allotted work while others have to wait for days or weeks and when finally given work are sent to far off places.

Regulatory Policy and IS workers: At present none of the legislation discussed above applies to the five occupations under study: domestic workers, IS sweepers, subcontract workers, khanawalis and fisherwomen. The first-three groups are casual wage workers and the last two are family-based and self-employment occupations. Thus different laws are likely to be necessary to provide protection and assistance to these differently situated occupations.

For subcontract workers (home-based piece rate workers) there are several possibilities. First, the existing legislation regulating minimum wages and shops and establishments could be amended to bring most home-based workers into the purview of these laws. Those who advocate this strategy argue that it is the simplest option and would enable resources to be concentrated, on educating workers about their rights. Others argue that there are so many problems with existing laws that a new law based entirely on the nature of the employer-employee relationship and of the work site for home-based workers would make it easier to win cases for those workers. This new law could be modeled on the Bidi Act. The National Commission on Self-employed Women recommended a third option for home-based workers: the setting up of Tripartite Boards modeled on the Private Security Guards Scheme described above. *Shram Shakti* (1988 : 116) gave several reasons for preferring tripartite boards to a protective act like the Bidi Act: a board would take over responsibility for both implementation and enforcement; it would do away with the necessity of establishing an employer-employee relationship; it would enable security of employment; and it would give home-based workers visibility.

Although sweepers and domestic workers are both casual wage workers, legal strategies for the two groups differ because of the different status of the employers in each case. In the case of sweepers in private buildings, it seems that once a private housing society is deemed an industry by the courts, then the existing labour laws will apply to them. Such an extension of the definition of industry is currently being argued in the courts. Domestic workers are one category which do not fit into any extended definition of labour laws. Hence, there is essential agreement that a new law is necessary for them.

For the khanawalis and fisherfolk—as self-employed and family based workers — traditional labour legislation based on the concept of an employer-employee relationship does not apply. The needs of these groups of workers revolve around social insurance issues—means of compensation if these workers are injured, become sick, or die during their working years, health benefits, and old age pensions—and around issues of small business — raw material, capital, markets. The first set of issues have yet to be addressed in a comprehensive way for any of the five groups of IS workers studied. The second set of issues has been addressed by the government through it policies on cooperatives and in its credit programmes for the self-employed discussed elsewhere in this chapter.

Cooperatives

A cooperatives society can be defined as an association in which members voluntarily join together to promote their common economic interests and distribute their surplus among themselves in proportion to their contribution made for earning that surplus (Tyagi 1968:7). Cooperatives were first introduced into India by the British during the early twentieth century for the purpose of providing credit to the peasants. From the beginning the state played a guiding role in the cooperative movement through the passage of central and provincial legislation — The Cooperative Credit Societies Acts of 1904 and 1912, and the Bombay Cooperative Credit Societies Act of 1925. By 1945-46 there were over 171,000 primary cooperative societies in India (Hough, 1950 : 276).

With the coming of independence the Indian Government continued the state supervision of cooperatives (guidance, audit, inspection, arbitration, liquidation, training of personnel) begun during the colonial period and expanded the state role in providing financial resources to cooperatives. On the basis of the recommendations of numerous committees, in 1958 the state established the National Cooperative Development Corporation, a new institution through which the state channeled most of its financial assistance (share capital contributions, loans, grants in aid and subsidies) to cooperatives.

In the *First Five Year Plan* (1953:80) the Indian Government expressed a commitment to cooperatives as a major aspect of development policy. The *Second Five Year Plan* announced a commitment to a "socialistic pattern of society" with an enhanced state role in industrialisation and an increasing role for cooperatives in the private sector. During the latter part of the 1950s the Planning Commission and Prime Minister Nehru for a time endorsed the idea of farm cooperatives loosely based on the Chinese model, but this idea was abandoned in 1959 in the face of fierce opposition from Congress party leaders (Frankel, 1978). Nevertheless the government commitment to expanding the reach of cooperatives and strengthening cooperatives continued although the emphasis was less on equality and more on efficiency by the beginning of the 1970s. The *Fourth Five Year Plan* (1970: 24) stated, "It is only when cooperative organisations embrace all activities from production, through credit, sale, supply, processing and storage to consumer stores and act as an integrated system that they can fully discharge their social and economic responsibilities."

Government policy in the fishing industry sought from the early days in independence to encourage the formation of cooperatives and to channel financial assistance through cooperatives. This policy followed the recommendations of the Fish Sub-Committee of the Agricultural Policy Committee (1944) which had recommended that state aid be given to fishermen and that it be given largely through cooperatives, which should give financial assistance, sell fishing requisites at a fair price, and should undertake marketing functions (Tyagi, 1968 : 22). These recommendations, including that cooperatives should be grouped together under central societies, Central Cooperative Banks should provide the finance for working capital, and the state should provide funds for improved boats; cold storage and transport, were largely adopted by the state after independence.

Thus state resources have been available since the 1940s to encourage the formation and growth of cooperatives in the fishing industry. This has not been the case in the other occupations under study. State resources have not necessarily resulted in economic improvement for the majority of fisherfolk. Government policies toward fish cooperatives resulted in an increase in the number, membership, and share capital of these cooperatives. However, there were numerous complaints of corruption and mismanagement in the operation of cooperatives resulting in massive losses by cooperatives.

Government Enquiries and Reports

Another way that the government has addressed the needs of certain categories of IS workers has been to set up enquiries or commissions to study the problems facing these groups and issue reports making recommendations. The establishment of such bodies indicates that the groups under study have some visibility and that representatives of the government are aware of the conditions that these workers face. Concrete action may not emerge from the recommendations issued by such bodies. In fact similar recommendations issued by a series of commissions over time indicate a pattern of government inaction. We shall briefly describe the government enquiries into the conditions of sweepers and of domestic workers.

Sweepers: Under the rubric of abolishing untouchability, a series of state and central government committees have been appointed since independence to look into the problems of sweepers. The first committee, appointed by the Government of Bombay in 1949, and chaired by V.N. Barve, the Scavengers' Living Conditions Enquiry Committee, issued its report in 1952, and subsequent committees in Mumbai and Maharashtra state included the Malkani committee in 1957, the Laud committee in 1973 and the Mehter committee in 1983 (Vivek, 1986). The Indian Government's Commissioner for Scheduled Castes and Scheduled Tribes issued annual reports which included discussion of the living and working conditions of sweepers. The National Commission of Labour, appointed in 1966, constituted a Committee to Study the Working and Service Conditions of Sweepers and Scavengers chaired by B. Pandya (National Commission on Labour 1969).

All of the reports made similar recommendations concerning the working conditions, length of work day, wages, and benefits of sweepers, and the reports focused almost exclusively on sweepers employed by government bodies. Abolishing the practice of carrying "night soil" and providing uniforms and protective clothing for cleaning public toilets were prominent themes of the reports. The reports advocated incorporating sweepers as permanent government employees, extending to them the provident fund and employees state insurance benefits that applied to government workers, and offering members of the sweeper communities opportunities of upward mobility through education and employment. The reports revealed that progress in achieving these objectives was uneven across the various states and even across municipalities within states.

Domestic workers: There are no central or state laws regulating domestic workers. However, there have been sporadic efforts in this direction. In 1959 the All India Domestic Workers Union approached the Prime Minister with demands for extending the Minimum Wages Act, the Shops and Establishment Act and the Industrial Disputes Act to domestic workers. That year a bill was introduced in Parliament providing for the registration of domestic workers and the regulation of hours, wages, and conditions of service, but it lapsed (Mehta, 1960).

Little more appears to have happened at the national level until the 1980s when several organisations raised issues. In 1980 the Catholic Bishop's Conference of India conducted a survey of domestic workers (Pereira, 1984). In response to lobbying efforts by the Gharelu Karamchari Association, New Delhi, demanding legal regulation of domestic service, the Labour Bureau, of the Union Ministry of Labour, did a study of domestic workers in Delhi and issued a report making recommendations regarding the sector in 1981. The report describes domestic service as an "ancient occupation" that "grew out of a feudal labour surplus migrating to the city" and notes that "due to omission of domestic service from any labour law, their working condition and hours of work are not regulated at present" (Labour Bureau, 1981). During the course of the survey information was collected on the personal condition, wages, hours of work, housing, welfare and medical facilities, and attitudes toward trade unions. Workers were also called upon to make suggestions which they felt were most appropriate for their cause and improvement in their working and living conditions.

The labour Bureau's 1981 report found that "Most of these servants belong to economically and socially backward communities of the society. Being illiterate and ignorant, they are open to exploitation by the employers," and recommended that domestic workers should receive statutory protection against possible exploitation by their employers. The report suggested that the following areas should be considered for regulation by law: working hours, rest periods, leaves, wages, written contracts, protection against arbitrary dismissal, settlement of disputes, registration with a government agency for the placement of domestic workers. The report also suggested the establishment of a welfare fund, night school facilities, and housing for domestic workers.

Government enquiries and commissions — concerning sweepers and domestic workers — have contributed visibility to the problems of these groups. However, the reports have a strong "welfare" orientation emphasising the disabilities of the groups and not their contributions as workers. The ensuing reports and recommendations have not necessarily led to laws or to laws addressing the needs of the entire group under consideration. Thus sweepers working for municipal governments have had their employment formalized, but those working in private buildings have not. There has been no legislation enacted to regulate domestic service.

Summing Up

In this chapter we have explored the policy context within which the five IS occupations under study operate. As a result of the Indian women's movement, the government has paid some attention recently to the problems of women IS workers. However, as of yet there are few laws protecting IS workers in the occupations in which women predominate. Most of the existing labour legislation does not apply to the IS. The government has paid some attention to the particular problems of sweepers and domestic workers as well. In the latter case no legislation has resulted. In the former case sweepers working for government bodies have experienced some improvement in working conditions, but private building sweepers have not been affected. The government has adopted some policies designed to benefit self-employed workers in the IS. Both the assistance toward cooperatives that pre-dated independence and the credit programmes for the self-employment poor that began in the 1970s are such policies. As far as IS workers are concerned, state regulatory policies (labour legislation) and distributive policies (mass banking and cooperatives' policies) are for the most part gender neutral on their face.

Nevertheless, in their implementation they have mainly reached male workers. Under certain circumstances organisations of self-employed women have been able to gain access to bank loans for women, have set up women's cooperatives, and have utilised labour legislation to gain protection for women workers. An analysis of the gendered nature of state policy is beyond the scope of this study, but it is a subject worth further examination. From the above review of the implications of state policies for the IS we can see that the government has differentially impacted the five occupations under study. What difference has that made for the five occupations and the organisations associated with them? As we will see in the next chapter, the fisherfolk have had four decades of government assistance to cooperatives. The khanawalis have had over ten years of access to bank loan programmes through the Annapurna Mahila Mandal. In contrast the sweepers, subcontract workers, and domestic workers have lacked the kinds of resources provided by governmental development policies and labour legislation. We will examine what difference this makes to the women workers in each occupation.

7

National Plan of Action on Children

Introduction

1. Right through the ages, care for children has been one of the causes to which Indian policy has remained committed. In independent India, this commitment was enshrined in our Constitutional provisions. The Constitution of India in its Directive Principles of State Policy pledges that "the State shall, in particular, direct its policy towards securing..... that the health and strength of workers, men and women, and the tender age of children, are not abused and that citizens are not forced by economic necessity to enter avocations unsuited to their age or strength; that children are given opportunities and facilities to develop in a healthy manner and in conditions of freedom and dignity and that childhood and youth are protected against exploitation and against moral and material abandonment." As a follow up to this commitment, Government of India adopted a National Policy for Children in 1974 which reaffirms the Constitutional provisions and declared that "it shall be the policy of the State to provide adequate services to children, both before and after birth and through the period of growth, to ensure their full physical, mental and social development. The State shall progressively increase the scope of such services so that, within a reasonable time, all children in the country enjoy optimum

conditions for their balanced growth." The specific measures to be adopted towards the attainment of these objectives are in Appendix-11.

2. Since independence human resource development programmes focussed on maternal and child health, nutrition and education have occupied an important place in India's efforts to raise the living standards of its poor. Successive Five Year Plans have provided the wherewithal to deal with these issues. In the last decade of this century, dramatic technological development particularly in health, nutrition and related spheres have opened up new vistas of opportunities for redeeming our age-old pledges to the cause of children. It is against this backdrop that India joined the comity of nations in the successive reaffirmations of global commitment to the cause of children in 1989-90. The UN Convention on the Rights of the Child in November 1989, the World Conference on Education for All at Jomtien in March 1990, the global consultation on Water and Sanitation in September, 1990, the World Summit on Children in the autumn of 1990 and the SAARC Summit on Children soon after the World Summit were all part of this reaffirmation process which transcended national barriers. India is a signatory to the World Declaration (September 1990) in the Survival, Protection and Development of Children and the Plan of Action for implementing it.

3. This National Plan of Action represents India's response to the unprecedented opportunities which the nineties decade has ushered in both through technology as well as a global ambience for redeeming India's age-old pledges. This Plan of Action identifies quantifiable targets in terms of major as well as supporting sectoral goals (detailed in Appendix-I of this Plan of Action) representing the needs and aspirations of almost over 300 million children

of India in the spheres of health, nutrition, education and related aspects of social support.

Situation of Children

4. Overall, basic indicators on children show a positive trend. For example, the infant mortality rate fell almost steadily from 146 per 1000 live births in 1960 to 80 per 1000 live births in 1990. The prevalence of severe and moderate degrees of malnutrition among children declined for the period 1974 to 1989. Primary school enrolment rates increased from 38 per cent in 1951 to 94 per cent in 1989. The availability of drinking water in rural areas improved significantly and by the end of the VII Plan (1989-90) 80 per cent of the population had been provided with potable water sources.

5. Major problems however, remain intertwined with the factors of poverty. For instance, about 30 per cent of the children born each year have low birth weight. The major causes of infant mortality viz. diarrhoea, pneumonia, neonatal tetanus and measles, are often aggravated by malnutrition. Protein-energy malnutrition affect about 52.5 per cent of all children below six years, with approximately a tenth of them suffering from severe malnutrition. Deficiency in Vitamin A causes, possibly among other adverse effects, an estimated 40,000 new cases of nutritional blindness each year. Some 70 per cent of women of child-bearing age suffer from chronic anaemia. Iodine deficiency is more widespread than hitherto suspected.

6. While there is a primary school in nearly all villages, problems remain in basic education, including lack of access to school, low achievement, high drop-out and repeater rates and severe disparities between socio-economic groups, geographic regions, rural and urban areas and between the boys and girls. While, Since 1951, the basic education

system has grown into one of the largest in the world with an enrolment, in 1989, of about 131 million children reaching out to about 94 per cent of the population, the retention has remained unsatisfactory with a drop out rate of 45 per cent for classes I-V and 60 per cent for classes I-VIII. At the end of the 1980's the overall picture shows that the gross enrolment ration for primary education has reached about 100 per cent however, the major reviews have advocated that targets for universalisation of elementary education should no longer be set in terms of additional enrolments for the country as a whole; disaggregated target setting policy has to be followed.

7. Inadequacy in the availability of safe drinking water, improper disposal of human excreta, solid and liquid water leading to unfavourable environmental conditions and lack of personal hygiene have been one of the major causes of disease and disability among children. In 13 States drinking water sources, are contaminated with excess fluoride causing thousands of children affected with dental and skeletal fluorosis. Excess nitrate in drinking water sources which might cause, Blue baby to children, is also observed in a number of States. About 15 lakh children die due to dehydration caused by Diarrhoea. As regards sanitation, the situation continues to be unsatisfactory as only about 3 per cent of the rural households are provided with low cost on-site human excreta disposal facilities as in 1990. Therefore, ensuring drinking water quality and strengthening its supportive linkages with health, and sanitation remain major challenges.

8. Children in especially difficult circumstances are without adequate family support and they may not be accessible through regular services. The rapid urbanisation, increased rural urban migration do have an adverse effect on children.

9. The situation of girls and boys differs significantly according to most indicators, particularly in the norther States.

10. The state of children hinges on the conditions of women. Most social indicators, including the sex ratio (929 females per 1000 males) and literacy (39 for females and 64 for males for all ages), point to the depressed situation of women. Socio-cultural bases, combined with poverty, weight heavily on women who marry early and bear children young, and who work excessively long hours in the home and outside, with unequal access to health and nutrition, educational and other opportunities, as well as insufficient legal protection and social and political participation.

11. The goals for children are promoted necessarily within the broader framework of national development planning. The key social development objectives of the 8th Five Year Plan (1992-97), are population control, employment generation and basic human needs particularly health care, literacy including elementary education and drinking water which is closely linked to sanitation.

12. Most of the recommendations of the World Summit for children contained in the Plan of Action for Survival, Protection and Development of Children were found relevant however, wherever these appeared to be too ambitious or beyond the resources likely to be available for these sectors, have been modified.

I. Health

A. Child Health

I.A.1. Major Goal: Reduction of infant mortality rate to less than 60 per thousand live births and reduction of child mortality rate to less than 10 by 2000 A.D.

I.A.1.1 Objectives

(i) Eradication of poliomyelitis by the year 2000;

(ii) Elimination of neonatal tetanus by 1995;

(iii) Reduction by 95 per cent in measles deaths and reduction by 90 per cent of measles cases compared to pre-immunisation levels by 1995;

(iv) Achievement and maintenance of high level of immunisation coverage at a level of 100 per cent of infants and against tetanus for women of child bearing age;

(v) Reduction by 50 per cent in deaths due to diarrhoea in children under the age of 5 years and 25 per cent of diarrhoea in incidence rate;

(vi) To endeavour to reduce mortality rates due to ARI among children under 5 by 40 per cent by 2000 A.D. from the present level.

I.A.1.2. Strategies

The basic instruments for achieving the stated objectives are.

I.A.1.2.1. Objective

Eradication of poliomyelitis by the year 2000 A.D.

Activities

(a) Strengthening of the existing primary health care infrastructure.

(b) Intensification of mortality/morbidity specific interventions by using the opportunity created by the Universal Immunisation Programme (UIP) in terms of continued contact with the mothers and young children for implementing a UIP Plus package of services combining immunisation with other basic

MCH interventions, progressively with view to universalising this package by 2000 A.D. The components of this package would be:

For Young Children

Newborn Care, (below 3 years): Primary immunisation by 12 months. Administration of Vitamin 'A' Pneumonia therapy and control of diarrhoeal diseases.

For Mothers

Antenatal Care, Immunisation against tetanus. Anaemia control during pregnancy. Screening and referral of high risk cases, care at birth and promoting spacing and timing of births.

I.A.1.2.2. Objective

Elimination of neonatal tetanus by 1995.

Activities

The thrust would be control of vaccine preventable diseases and documentation of 'zero' levels of neonatal tetanus in a phased manner. The elimination of neonatal tetanus implies immunisation combined with better birth practices, with safe motherhood.

I.A.I.2.3. Objective

Reduction by 95 per cent in measles deaths and reduction by 90 per cent of measles cases compared to pre-immunisation levels by 1995.

Activities

(a) Specific measures will be taken to consolidate and maintain levels of immunisation coverage, and to step up immunisation where coverage is low.

(b) The immunisation services will be reprogrammed

towards polio eradication, elimination of neo-natal tetanus and decrease in cases as well as deaths due to measles.

(c) Appropriate measures will be taken towards the provision of essential items in adequate quantities such as vaccines, syringes and needles and immunisation cards so that coverage level and quality of services do not drop.

(d) Field supervision would be improved.

I.A.1.2.4. Objective

To achieve and maintain Immunisation coverage at a level of 100 per cent of infants.

Activities

(a) "UIP Plus" package consisting of immunisation, control of diarrhoeal diseases, pneumonia diagnosis and therapy. Vitamin 'A' and Newborn care will be implemented.

(b) Initiatives will be taken to ensure that essential supplies and drugs are made available regularly and on time at health units.

(c) Steps will be taken to create demand for the package of services for children.

(d) Inter-sectoral programmes such as integrated Child Development Services (ICDS), Urban Basic Services (UBS) and Development of Women and Children in Rural Areas.(DWCRA) will be activated for reaching young children and women with set of complementary interventions for improved mother and child survival and health.

(e) Emphasis will be given to decentralised planning and implementation using the district as a Unit.

(f) A holistic approach aimed at better health of women and children through affordable means, by adopting 'high risk' criteria will be the strategy.

I.A.1.2.5. Objective

Fifty per cent reduction in deaths due to diarrhoea in children under the age of 5 years and 25 per cent reduction in the diarrhoea incidence rate.

Activities

(a) The training communication, supply and logistic support for village level care for diarrhoeal diseases will be made operational university in districts in a phased manner.

(b) Case management will be improved at hospital referral centres, more specially, district hospitals and primary health centres.

(c) Diarrhoea Training Units at Medical College Hospitals will be set up.

(d) Intensive efforts will be made to network with non-governmental organisations and educate the people.

(e) Several village level outlets will be used for provision of ORS and a communication campaign will be launched to create a demand for ORS.

(f) Special emphasis will be given to home management of diarrhoea-mothers and families will be trained by both interpersonal as well as mass media to adopt appropriate practices for correct case management at home and timely referral.

(g) The wide-spread infrastructure of other programmes like rural development, urban development and ICDS, will be used to extend the outreach for education of mothers on appropriate home care.

I.A.1.2.6. Objective

To endeavour to reduce mortality rates due to ARI among children under-5 by 40 per cent by 2000 A.D. from the present level.

Activities

(a) The rational use of antibiotics for treatment would be ensured in a phased manner in all the districts.

(b) Training of the PHC doctors and female Para-medical Health Workers.

(c) Communication support to the Programme from within and outside the health sector to enhance 'use of services.

(d) Action for promoting home management of mild infection and timely referral to a health worker or an appropriate facility.

(e) Proper care management by health workers involving correct assessment and treatment

B. Maternal Health

I.B.1. Major Goal

Between 1990 & the year 2000, reduction of maternal mortality rate by half.

I.B.1.1. Objectives for Women's Health and Education.

(i) Special attention to health and nutrition of the female child and to pregnant and lactating women;

(ii) Access by all couples to information and services to prevent pregnancies that are too early, too closely spaced, too late or too many;

(iii) Access by all pregnant women to prenatal care, trained attendants during child birth and referral facilities for high risk pregnancies and obstetric emergencies;

(iv) Universal access to primary education with special emphasis for girls and accelerated literacy programmes for women.

Strategies for Objectives (i) to (iii)

(i) A minimum of three ante-natal check-ups during pregnancy will be arranged to detect high risk groups and for complete immunisation.

(ii) Pregnant women will be immunised against tetanus.

(iii) There will be anaemia control activities during pregnancy,

(iv) Spacing and timing of births will be promoted,

(v) Specific measures, necessary for consolidation and maintenance of high levels of immunisation coverage and stepping up the coverage wherever they are identified to be low, will be taken up.

(vi) Health care units will be strengthened as first level referral to deal with obstetric emergencies.

(vii) Traditional birth attendants would be trained/ retrained to ensure that deliveries are conducted by IBAs.

(viii) Measures will be taken for skill development of medical and paramedical workers for institutionalising the referral systems for management of obstetric complications.

(ix) The work routines of the key worker i.e. the Auxiliary Nurse and Midwife (ANM) would be rationalised be re-defining her tasks so as to include only those activities that will result in preventing deaths.

(x) There would be increasing involvement of Voluntary Workers at village, level, so that ANM is able to concentrate on delivery of services, such as immunisation, Vitamin A Prophylaxis, iron and

Folk Acid and on the management of cases of diarrhoea, anaemia, pneumonia and pregnancy.

(xi) District will be the Unit for planning and management of services. District plans would be developed based on the infrastructure and facilities for providing services. It will be the unit for supply, social mobilisation and monitoring.

(xii) Steps will be taken to create demand for the package of services for mothers and children.

(xiii) Girls between the age of 13 and 20 shall be reached through an exposure programme which covers the basic of safe motherhood and timing of births.

(xiv) Tetanus toxide will be promoted during the pre-pregnancy period for adolescents and this event will be used to identify anaemia among adolescents and to appraise their health status.

(xv) Activities to promote health growth of adolescent girls will be implemented, such as supplementary iron.

I.B. 1.2. Objective

Universal access to Primary Education with special emphasis for girls and accelerated literacy programme for women.

Activities

(a) Provision of additional infrastructure will be made.

(b) Efforts will be made to enhance the self image and self-confidence of women and to enable them to recognise their contribution to the economy as producers and workers.

(c) Provide women with the necessary support structures and an informal learning environment to create time for education.

(d) To create an environment which young girls and adolescent girls working in their homes in agriculture and elsewhere get an opportunity for formal education.

(e) Provision of primary education facilities in unserved or undeserved areas as alternative models for education such as use of village women, low cost hostel facilities, widening primary education opportunities for girls, increasing the number of women teachers, providing residential accommodation for women teachers.

(f) Create Child Care Service to release girls from sibling care responsibilities for participating in educational activities.

(g) Improve access to drinking water and sanitation facilities within the community as a whole so as to lessen the burden of household chores among girls and women.

(h) Create non-formal educational facilities as an alternative to formal schools.

(i) Community mobilisation and involvement efforts.

(j) Provision of suitable incentives and facilities for girls.

Nutrition

II. 1. Major Goal

Between 1990 and the year 2000 A.D. reduction in severe and moderate malnutrition among under-5 children by half.

Objectives

(i) Reduction in severe as well as moderate malnutrition among under-5 children by half of 1990 levels,

(ii) Reduction in incidence of low birth weight (2.5 kg. or less) babies,

(iii) Reduction of iron deficiency anaemia in women,

(iv) Control of iodine deficiency disorders,

(v) Control of Vitamin A deficiency and its consequences including blindness,

(vi) Empowerment of all women to breast-feed their children exclusively for four to six months and to continue breast-feeding with complementary food, well into the second year,

(vii) Growth promotion and its regular monitoring to be institutionalised by the end of the 1990s,

(viii) Dissemination of knowledge and supporting services to increase food production to ensure household food security.

II. 1.2.1. Objective

Reduction in severe, as well as moderate malnutrition among under-5 children by half of 1990 levels..

Activities

(a) Expansion of nutritional intervention net through ICDS so as to cover all vulnerable children in the age group of 0-6 years.

(b) A concerted effort to bring about appropriate behavioural changes among the mothers through existing programmes such as the Integrated Child Development Services (ICDS), safe motherhood, Urban Basic Services (UBS), Development of Women and Children in Rural Areas (DWCRA) and programmes of Food and Nutrition Board.

(c) Improvement in growth monitoring between the age group 0-3 years with closer involvement of mothers to be taken.

(d) Encouraging small family norms and adequate spacing through intensive family welfare and motivational measures so that availability of food is sufficient

(e) Involving the community in the identification of problems and management of nutrition programmes and related interventions such as health education, involvement of women in food production and processing activities and other employment generation activities.

(f) Emphasis on women's employment and education particularly nutrition and health education.

(g) Convergence of services by strengthening linkages between the concerned sectors like agriculture, food, health, women and child development, education, rural development, urban development, etc.

(h) Creation of conducive environment by providing safe drinking water, clean environment, immunisation service, health care etc.

II. 1.2.2. Reduction in Incidence of Low Birth Weight (2.5 kg or less) Babies

(a) Nutritional communication will be developed to create greater awareness of nutritional problems and their solutions amongst the general public.

(b) Nutrition education, will be closely linked to activities like immunisation, Oral Rehydration Therapy, promotion of breast-feeding, birth spacing and female education.

(c) Appropriate low cost nutrition foods for Supplementary Feeding Programme at ICDS Project areas will be developed.

(d) Correct dietary habits for improving nutritional levels through behavioural change will be promoted.

(e) Ante-natal and post-natal care to women for preventing low birth weight babies will be provided.

(f) Ensuring better nutritional coverage of expectant mothers right from the 1st trimester for the major period of lactation.

II. 1.23. Reduction of Iron Deficiency (Anaemia) in Women

(a) Consumption of iron-rich foods will be improved and promoted through Integrated Child Development Services (ICDS), Maternal and Child Health (MCH), Urban Basic Services (UBS) & Development of Women and Children in Rural Areas (DWCRA) Programmes.

(b) "UIP Plus" package will include control of iron deficiency anaemia through ensuring iron supplements to pregnant women.

(c) All pregnant women and 50 per cent of young anaemic children will be covered with iron and folic acid.

(d) Improved quality, packaging and distribution of iron and folic acid tablets will be ensured.

II. 1.2.4. Control of iodine deficiency disorder

(a) A comprehensive strategy for control of IDD will be developed. The distribution and consumption of iodised salt will be promoted through various channels.

(b) Research and development studies will be sponsored to assess the feasibility of double fortification of salt with iron and iodine.

(c) The strategy for communication and training as well as management information system for MCH services and ICDS will include component of control of iodine deficiency disorders.

(d) Linkages with contact points such as the immunisation programme and ICDS will be developed to ensure maximum coverage of control of iodine deficiency.

II. 1.2.5. Control of Vitamin A deficiency and its consequences including blindness.

(a) National Prophylaxis programmes for control of Vitamin-A deficiency will be effectively implemented.

(b) Emphasis will be placed on efforts to improve diets rich in Vitamin-A.

(c) Capacity to produce more Vitamin-A concentrates will be expanded further with a view of effectively implement national policy on Vitamin-A programmes.

(d) Administration of Vitamin-A to all children between nine months to three years, as well as treatment doses to infants and young children following each attack of diarrhoea, measles and acute respiratory infection will be ensured.

(e) Utilisation of existing nutrition, health services will be further improved.

(f) Breast-feeding and better infant feeding practices will be promoted.

II. 1.2.6. Empowerment of all women to breastfeed their children exclusively for four to six months and to continue breast-feeding with complementary food, well into the second year.

Activities

(a) Awareness amongst functionaries of various programmes such as Integrated Child Development Services (ICDS), Urban Basic Services (UBS), Development of Women and Children in Rural Areas

(DWCRA) workers, health workers, doctors, families and mothers will be created for promotion of breastfeeding.

(b) Health workers will be trained to promote appropriate lactation management and breastfeeding.

(c) The communication strategy for child survival and health will include breastfeeding as an integral component.

II. 1.2.7. Growth promotion and its regular monitoring to be institutionalised by the end of the 1990s.

Activities

(a) Growth promotion and its regular monitoring will be an integral component of health and nutrition programme. Involvement of women in growth monitoring would be encouraged.

(b) Gross root level workers of Integrated Child Development Services (ICDS), Urban Basic Services (UBS) & Maternal and Child Health (MCH) will be trained in growth monitoring.

II. 1.2.8. Dissemination of knowledge and supporting services to increase food, production to ensure household food security.

Activities

(a) Ensured nutritional adequacy by increasing the production and increasing availability of nutritionally rich food.

(b) Utilisation of the available food resources through the application of effective food technology.

(c) Food availability to ail-specially weaker sections to ensure household food security.

(d) Strengthening of Public Distribution System and Incorporation of nutritional consideration in Public Distribution System and in all poverty alleviation programmes.

III. Water and Sanitation

III. 1. Major Goal

Universal access to safe drinking water and improved access to sanitary means of excreta disposal.

III. 1.1. The norms for providing drinking water in rural areas and those pertaining to sanitation are as follows:

Water

(i) To arrange potable water source within a distance of one Km. horizontal and 50 metres elevation difference.

(ii) One spot source or standpost for 100/150 persons.

Sanitation

A package linked with the demand and need and with a differential beneficiary contribution.

III. 1.2. Objectives

(i) To provide the entire rural population with potable water supplies @.40 lpcd.

(ii) To cover 10 per cent of population with sanitary facilities by the year 1997.

(iii) To eradicate guineaworm disease by 1995.

(iv) To provide safe water with fluoride content within tolerable limits by the year 2000 A.D.

Activities

Water

(i) Coverage of remaining no-source villages.

(ii) Coverage of habitation with special emphasis on Scheduled Castes (SC) Scheduled Tribes (ST).

(iii) Augmentation of service level,

(iv) Improved operation and maintenance,

(v) Quality improvement.

(vi) Water resource management and prevention of failure of sources,

(vii) Health Education, Community Participation and Awareness programme.

Sanitation

(i) Taking sanitation as a package.

(ii) Adoption of a demand and need based approach to make the programme a people's movement.

(iii) Establishment/Strengthening of State/District Sanitation Cell.

(iv) Intensive district programming.

(v) Development of appropriate delivery system.

(vi) Adoption of an appropriate IEC strategy,

(vii) Empowerment of women on improved sanitary practices.

(viii) Co-ordination with other related programmes.

(ix) Involvement of community, voluntary organisations and NGO's.

(x) R & D to develop appropriate area specific low cost technology to suit different geo-hydrological conditions.

IV. Education

IV.l. Major Goal

Universal enrolment, retention, minimum level of learning, reduction of disparities and universalisation of effective access of schooling.

IV. 1.1 Objectives

(a) Universal enrolment of all children including girls, using both full time formal schools & part time non-formal arrangements.

(b) Reduction of drop-out rate between class I to V and I to VIII from the existing 45 per cent and 60 per cent to 20 per cent and 40 per cent respectively.

(c) Achievement of minimum level of learning by approximately all children at the primary level and introduction of this concept at the upper primary stage on large scale.

(d) Reduction in disparities by emphasis on girl's education and special measures for children belonging to Scheduled Castes/Scheduled Tribes (SC/ST).

(e) Expansion of Early Childhood Development activities including appropriate low cost family and community based interventions.

(f) Universalisation of effective access to schooling. The two broad strategy frames for reaching the targets are:

  (i) Micro-planning through people's participation and decentralisation; and

  (ii) Introducing Minimum Levels of Learning (MLL) in schools. Micro-planning would be area specific, population specific through mobilising community participation, decentralising educational administration, reorienting and strengthening local administrative and resource support systems, ascertaining educational requirements of the area, bringing to school all children who can be enrolled, seeing that all children regularly and actually participate in primary education and planning for the improvement of the schools. Minimum levels of learning strategy focuses on learning acquisition in schools & outcomes and is proposed to be implemented through an assessment of the existing level of learning achievement; a definition of the MLL for the area and the time frame for achieving it; reorientation of teaching practices to competency based teaching; introduction of evaluation of student learning; review of textbooks and re-revision, if required and the provision of inputs to improve learning acquisition to the MLL including provision of physical facilities, teacher training, supervision, evaluation etc.

Objectives

(i) Universal enrolment of all children including girls, using both full-time formal schools and part-time non-formal arrangements.

(ii) Reduction of drop-out rate between classes I to V and I to VIII from the existing 45 per cent and 60 per cent to 20 per cent and 40 per cent respectively.

(iii) Achievement of minimum level of learning by approximately all children at the primary level and introduction of this concept at the upper primary stage on a large scale.

Activities

(i) Seek people's participation by arousing them to the need for education, creating a sense of responsibility towards children's education and empowering them to take accountability of the school system.

(ii) Community mobilisation and environment building will use folk and traditional media, people-to-people discussions, group meetings etc.

(iii) Village Education Committees (VEC) will be formed in each village, with adequate representation of women and the disadvantaged groups, to interact with teachers, provide support to the school, ensure regular participation of all children through parental motivation and take accountability over the running of the school.

(iv) Efforts will be made to involve suitable NGOs or field level organisations/project management and to strengthen them adequately for such provision of support to the VEC. Capacity building at local levels will be an essential activity in all areas adopting the microplanning strategy.

(v) In the next 5 years, efforts will be made to shift educational planning to the district level, by setting up District Boards of Education and District Institutes of Education and Training (DIETs).

(vi) An effective MIS will be created to provide information required for decision making, planning and management to the district levels and information for monitoring district plans of the State and national levels.

(vii) The accent during the next 5 years will be upon opening of new primary schools according to the norm in the unserved habitation, and the provision of non-formal education programmes for smaller habitations and for children who cannot benefit from the school system.

(viii) In order to increase enrolment at the upper primary stage, the infrastructure at the upper primary stage will be considerably expanded.

(ix) The existing norms of providing an upper primary school within 3 km walking distance, for all practical purposes, denies education at this level to a large section of girls. This norm will be relaxed and the existing ratio between primary and upper primary schools will be improved to 1:2.

(x) Provisions will be made to add additional rooms and provide additional teachers to existing schools through the scheme of Operation Blackboard and the existing norm for the minimum-2 classrooms and 2 teachers-will be raised successively.

(xi) Non-formal education (NFE) will be developed as a complementary system to the formal education system, such that there will be parallel administrative apparatus for NFE; greater attention to the interests of the learner, and its quality will be comparable with formal system and conform to the MLLs laid down for the primary stage.

(xii) Mechanisms will be developed for entry from non-formal to the formal system and vice-versa.

(xiii) The NFE programme will include a substantial enhancement in costs per learner, on the reasoning that it is not possible to reach out to the marginalised groups with marginalised funding.

(xiv) In order to ensure that regular in-service training and academic supervision is provided to teachers, a beginning will be made to create Teachers' Centres for every cluster of 20-25 primary schools to provide a forum to teachers to get together, discuss issues, resolve common problems and receive academic guidance to build upon their capacities and skills.

(xv) A programme of in-service training of teachers will be coordinated by this block level team to infuse a level of competency in teachers to effectively transact curriculum and textual material.

(xvi) At the State level the existing Councils of Educational Research and Training (SCERT) will be restructured so that they become institutions principally for resource support to elementary education, non-formal education and early childhood education.

(xvii) Resource support through researches and studies will be encouraged by continuing support to Colleges of Teacher Education and Institutes of Advanced Studies in Education.

(xviii) District specific plans will be developed as projects, with specific activities, clearly defined responsibilities, definite time-schedules and district specific targets. Apart from effective UEE the goals of each project will include the reduction of existing disparities in educational access, the provision of alternative systems of comparable standards to the disadvantaged groups, bringing about a substantial improvement in the quality of schooling facilities, obtaining a genuine community involvement in running of schools, and building up local level capacity to ensure effective decentralisation of educational planning.

(xix) A monitoring system will be developed to obtain timely and reliable information on enrolment, retention, completion and achievement. In addition the qualitative monitoring of achievement will also be introduced.

Objective

For Reduction in Disparities: by Emphasis on girls' education, and Special measures for children belonging to Scheduled Castes/Scheduled Tribes (SC/ST).

Activities

(i) An effort will be made to provide a comprehensive system of incentives and support services for girls and children of the economically weaker sections of society.

(ii) A provision of services such as establishment of Day Care Centres for pre-school children and infants, provision of free uniforms, text books and stationary as attendance incentives to girls, coordination of support services such as drinking water, fodder and fuel.

(iii) A similar incentive as appropriate, will be provided in the non-formal system, also, in addition to provision of free text books and stationery to all NFE learners.

Objective

For Early Childhood Education:

Expansion of early childhood development activities including appropriate low-cost family and community based interventions.

Activities

(i) During the VIII Five Year Plan, the ICDS will be

expanded and will be the main scheme for early childhood activities.

(ii) The contribution of ICDS to basic education will be enhanced by adjusting it to school timings and by strengthening its educational component.

(iii) Other existing schemes for early childhood education will be improved so as to become holistic schemes providing nutrition and health care as well as education.

(iv) Emphasis and efforts will be made on training of personnel, production of sufficient play way learning material for children, creation of a system of monitoring and supervision; and development of effective rapport between ECCE and community and the primary school.

IV. 2. Major Goal

Achievement of adult literacy rate of 80 per cent (which is of mastery level) in the age group 15-35, with emphasis on female literacy.

Objective

Imparting of functional literacy so as to enable the learners to achieve self-reliance in literacy and numeracy, to make them aware of the causes of their deprivation and move towards amelioration of their condition through organisation and participation in the process of development, acquire skills to improve their economic status and general well-being and imbibe in themselves the values of national integration, conservation of the environment, women's equality, observance of small family, norms etc.

Activities

(i) Continuous environment building conducive to literacy through jathas, rallies, media and communication, traditional folk art forms etc. and securing a national consensus among all sections of the society including political parties, representatives of the people, etc.

(ii) Organising mass campaigns for total literacy which are area-specific, time-bound, volunteer-based, cost-effective and result-oriented in 345 districts of the country up to 1997.

(iii) Involving a large number of voluntary agencies in programmes relating to eradication of illiteracy in a campaign mode.

(iv) Increasing involvement of students in schools and colleges, nonstudent unemployed youth, youth clubs, teachers and representatives of other non-governmental organisations, etc. in literacy activities.

(v) Use of the new teaching/learning pedagogy evolved under the technique of Improved Pace and Content of Learning (IPCL) providing for reduced duration of learning, heightened motivation of learners and an in-built mechanism for self evaluation by the learners.

(vi) Strengthening of the academic and technical resource support to the programme by establishment of additional State Resource Centres, Regional Resource Centres, District Resource Units, etc.

(vii) Making adequate arrangements for training of all field functionaries and timely supply of teaching/learning material.

(viii) Developing, designing and patenting various techno-pedagogic imputs for improving the pace and quality of the programme by pursuing the findings of the scientific and technological research.

(ix) Imparting literacy to the learners in their spoken language and supply of district-specific and culture-specific teaching-learning material to heighten and sustain the motivation of the learners.

(x) Increasing emphasis on coverage of women learners by setting up of large number of adult education centres exclusively for women, involvement of women volunteers in substantial numbers, giving preference to women in the matter of appointment of Preraks of Jana Shikshan Nilayams and providing teaching-learning material relevant to the needs of women.

(xi) Launching of post-literacy campaigns immediately alter the conclusion of the total literacy campaigns so as to prevent the risk of the neoliterates relapsing into illiteracy.

(xii) Establishment of Jana Shikshan Nilayams for providing facilities of post literacy and continuing education in areas which are covered by the programmes other than total literacy campaigns.

(xiii) Establishing linkages with other developmental programmes like health & family welfare, conservation of environment, agriculture, rural development, etc.

(xiv) Evolving suitable mechanisms for continuous monitoring and evaluation of the programme at various levels.

(xv) Continuous research on Adult Education Programmes of all descriptions to make the Programmes more meaningful and effective.

V. Children in Especially Difficult Circumstances

V. 1. Major Goal

Improved protection of children in especially difficult circumstances.

Objective

Provision of protection of children in especially difficult circumstances and tackle the root cause leading to such situations. This would include children in following categories; physically handicapped; mentally handicapped; drug addicts, victims of natural and man-made disasters, refugee children, street children, slum & migrant children, orphans & destitutes; children suffering from AIDS, children of parents with AIDS & AIDS orphans, children of prostitutes & child prostitutes & juvenile delinquents and child labour.

Activities

(a) Efforts will be made to build linkages between existing Child Care Institutions and communities and society at large for greater community participation for children in especially difficult circumstances.

(b) The staff of institutions and implementing bodies will receive pre and in-service training.

(c) Interventions for street children and other children in difficult circumstances will be made with active support of the Municipal Bodies, Health Department, Education Department etc. through relevant programmes in the social service sector.

(d) To strengthen prevention of Child Labour, emphasis will be on compulsory education for all children and on strengthening anti-poverty and development programmes and focussing them on at risk families.

(e) Voluntary Organisations will be assisted to undertake projects for welfare and development of children in especially difficult circumstances.

(f) National Child Labour Policy 1987 will be taken up more vigorously for implementation.

V. 2. Goal

To assist children affected by one or more disabilities, having no access to proper rehabilitative services and especially to lift up the status of those most marginalised.

Strategy

To set in motion advocacy and services for disabled children in two main phases;

(i) to help people understand that disabilities are a commonly occurring phenomenon with specific causes and that their own endeavour can help reduce both the incidence of disability and its severity, and

(ii) to ensure that people recognise that rehabilitation is possible and to help inform them about how to receive those services.

Activities

There will be four main priority areas for work in child disability fields:

(i) To enable and to mobilise all central areas in social services beginning at the community level to assist in the process of primary detection, prevention, and rehabilitation;

(ii) To create a cadre of very well trained workers ranging in expertise from early detection and rehabilitation at the community level, to those who have the most up-to-date skills; to make sure that the best quality care is made available at the most appropriate level for disabled people.

(iii) Communication efforts needed at all levels will be made to alert people to the fact the disabilities need not become handicaps, that they can be prevented, that when they occur they need not unnecessarily prevent an individual from being a full member of the community. Good communication campaigns which can also deeply change people's attitude towards disablement and towards people who are affected by a disability or handicap will be launched. Communications campaigns and strategies that can ensure that all of those who can affect and improve the quality of services available to the disabled people see this as an appropriate priority and take suitable action.

(iv) To support and encourage the various institutions, both government and nongovernmental which are putting new ideas into practice in the field of disability. Support would be given to these institutions to help them implement them and to measure the impact and effect of these strategies.

V. 3.

Amongst children who are neglected, abandoned or rendered destitute a large number of children are handicapped and special provisions need to be made for such children. The aims and objectives for the handicapped children would, therefore, be:

(i) to provide residential facilities to children suffering from severe/profound mental retardation or cerebral palsy;

(ii) to provice facilities for care and protection, maintenance, treatment and rehabilitation for such, children;

(iii) to provide pre-vocational training in accordance with the needs and capabilities of the children; and

(iv) to workout development based approaches, strategies, programmes and services for the children.

VI. Girl Child

VI. 1. Objective

To remove the gender bias and to improve the status of the girl child in society so as to provide her with equal opportunities for her survival and development to her full potential.

Activities

Keeping in view the prevailing gender bias and disadvantaged status of the female child, special programmes and interventions directed at the girl child are required to ensure her an equal status and a better quality of life. These should take into account her peculiar social, cultural and economic mileau which would require special-strategies and interventions. The Action Plan for the SAARC Decade ill of the Girl Child includes programmes of both advocacy and action in the developmental areas of health, education, welfare etc. A special focus will be ** child survival. The Action Plan is proposed to be implemented in close collaboration with the concerned Central Ministries, State Governments and Non-governmental Organisations.

VIl. Adolescent Girls

VII. l. Objective

Programme for the adolescent girls should embrace a whole range of activities, such as nutrition, health, education, health and nutrition education, recreation, upgradation of home-based skills and promotion of her decision making capability as adolescent girls who are one of the most critical human resource, particularly at the village level with the following objectives:

(i) to cover girls in the age group of 11 to 18 years;

(ii) to improve the nutritional and health status of girls in this age groups;

(iii) to provide them the required literacy and numeracy skills, through the non-formal stream of education, to stipulate a desire for more social exposure and knowledge and to help them improve their decision making capabilities, especially on issues regarding their future.

(iv) to train and equip the girls to improve and upgrade home based skills;

(v) to promote awareness of health, hygiene, nutrition and family welfare, home management and child care, to take all other measures as would facilitate their marrying only after attaining the age of 18 and, if possible, even later.

VIII. Children and the Environment

VIII. 1. Objective

To conserve and protect environment so that it is conducive to the health and well being of the children.

Activities

Awareness should be created among children regarding important of protection of the environment and they should be encouraged to participate in activities aimed at prosection of environment.

IX. Women

Development of Women is intertwined with that of Children and constitutes a vital component, of a country's human resource development Therefore, these two target groups deserve special treatment in addition to their legitimate share from all other general developmental programmes. The major objective of all the developmental programmes, both women-specific and women-related has, therefore, been to ensure a state of 'well-being' and children particularly those of the weaker sections of society. In this direction, a special emphasis will be on developing Women's potential and main-streaming them into the national development process through enhanced access to skill development and income generation opportunities which are expected to provide not only the desired economic independence but also to help improve their quality of life as well as that of their families and children. The ongoing 27-beneficiary oriented schemes for women in the major developmental areas of health, education, family welfare, employment, rural and urban development, science and technology, etc. will be further strengthened by adding additionalities like safe motherhood, child survival, employment and income generation, etc.

X. Advocacy and People's Participation

Advocacy for the child as everyone's concern and advocacy with policy makers, planners, programme implementors at national and international levels for focus on the child will be integral to the achievement of the goals. In order to implement the plan of children, voluntary organisations, local bodies, religious institutions and political parties would be mobilised for achieving the above mentioned goals. All channels of communication, formal and informal including mass media would be utilised for wider dissemination of the urgent need for achieving goals concerning children.

XI. Resources

Efforts would be made to mobilise adequate financial resources for implementation of the National Plan of Action on Children.

XII. Monitoring and Evaluation

To monitor the quality of service and the attainment

of goals, the country will select appropriate indicators for each of the stated goals, to be monitored by the relevant sectors at regular intervals. For this the following activities will be pursued:

(i) Development and monitoring of critical indicators for measuring progress towards the goals;

(ii) For participatory monitoring of programme coverage and results at the community level; and

(iii) Action research and field studies relevant to the achievement of the goals for children.

Appendices

APPENDIX—II

INSTITUTES OF SOCIAL WORK EDUCATION IN INDIA

West Bengal

1. Indian Institute of Social Welfare and Business Management, Calcutta University
2. Palli Sangthan Vibhag (Rural Reconstructions College), Vishwa Bharati University, Shantiniketan 731235

Uttar Pradesh

1. Institute of Social Sciences, Agra
2. Kashi Vidyapith, Varanasi 221002
3. Lucknow University, Badshah Bagh, Lucknow 226007

Delhi

1. University of Delhi, Delhi 110007
2. Jamia Millia Islamia, Jamia Nagar, New Delhi 110025

Rajasthan

1. Tirpude College of Social Work, Pratap Nagar, Rajasthan University
2. Rajasthan Vidyapeeth, Udaipur 313001

Haryana

1. Kurukshetra University, Guru Nanak Khalsa College, Yamuna Nagar, Department of Social work, Kurukshetra 132119

Gujarat

1. Gujarat Vidyapeeth, Ashram Road, Ahmedabad 380014
2. M.S. University of Baroda, Vadodara 390002

Madhya Pradesh

1. Devi Ahilya Vishwavidyalaya (M.A), 169, Ravindra Nath Tagore Marg, Indore 452001
2. Vikram University, Kothi Road, Ujjain 456010

Maharashtra

1. Ahmed Nagar College, Poona University, Ahmednagar
2. Adhyapak Shikshan Mandali Arts & Commerce College, Taloda
3. College of Social Work, Nirmala Niketan (Bombay University), Mumbai
4. College of Social Work, Vasant Vihar, Jawahar Colony, Aurangabad (Aurangabad University)
5. Chhatrapati Shahu Central Institute of Business of Business Education and Research, Kolhapur
6. Karve Institute of Social Science, Poona University, Pune
7. Tata Institute of Social Sciences, P.O.8313, Sion-Trombay Road, Deonar, Mumbai 400088
8. Amravati University, near Tapowan, Amravati 440602
9. University of Bombay, M.G. Road, Fort, Mumbai 400032

10. University of Poona, Ganeshkind, Pune 411007
11. Marathawada University, Aurangabad 431004
12. Nagpur University, near Maharaja Bagh, M.G marg, Nagpur 440001

Karnataka

1. Central College, Bangalore University, Bangalore
2. Mysore University, Mysore
3. School of Social Work, Mangalore, (Mangalore University)
4. Karnataka University, Pavat Nagar, Dharwad 580003
5. Mangalore University, University Campus, Mangalagangothri 574119
6. Bangalore University, Jnana Bharati, Bangalore 560056
7. Gulbarga University, Jnana Ganga, Gulbarga 585106
8. Christ College,Hosur Road, Bangalore - 29,India.Phone Number: 25536280.

Andhra Pradesh

1. Andhra University, Waltair 530003
2. Sri Krishnadevaraya University, Sri Venkateshwarapuram, Anantpur 515003
3. Sri Padmavati Mahila Vishavidyalayam, Tirupati 517502

Kerala

1. Loyola College of Social Sciences, Trivandrum (Kerala University)
2. Rajgiri College of Social Sciences, Kalamassery, Gandhiji University

3. University of Kerala, P.O. University, Thiruvananthapuram 695034

Tamil Nadu

1. Bharathiar University, Post Maruthumalai Main Road, Coimbatore - 641 046
2. Madras School of Social Work, Egmore, Chennai
3. Bharathidasan Palkalai Perun, Tiruchirapalli 620024
4. Madurai Kamraj University Palkalai Nagar, Madurai 625021

APPENDIX—II

GLOBAL ACTION FOR WOMEN TOWARDS SUSTAINABLE AND EQUITABLE DEVELOPMENT

INTRODUCTION

(Section III, Chapter 1)

This programme area was prepared on the basis of a Preparatory Committee decision on women in environment and development in which the Preparatory Committee requested the Secretary-General of the Rio Conference "to ensure that key elements relating to women's critical economic, social and environmental contributions to sustainable development be addressed at the United Nations Conference on Environment and Development. It was emphasised that this was a distinct cross-cutting issue in addition to being mainstreamed in all the substantive work and documentation particularly Agenda 21, the Earth Charter and the Conventions." Other Agenda 21 programmes of special relevance to women included sustainable agriculture and rural development, freshwater resources, combating poverty, education and health. Recommendations from relevant meetings on women in environment and sustainable development also requested by the Preparatory Committee in are contained in UN document (A/CONF.ISI/PC/114).

Basis for action — Chapter 24*

24.1. The international community has endorsed several plans of action and conventions for the full, equal and beneficial integration of women in all development activities in particular the Nairobi Forward-looking Strategies for the Advancement of Women, which emphasise women's participation in national and international ecosystem management and control of environment degradation. Several conventions, including the Convention on the Elimination of All Forms of Discrimination against Women (General Assembly Resolution 34/180, annex) and Conventions of ILO and UNESCO have also been adopted to end gender-based discrimination and ensure women's access to land and other resources, education and safe and equal employment. Also relevant are the UNICEF 1990 World Declaration on the Survival, Protection and Development of Children and its Plan of Action. Effective implementation of these programmes will depend on the active involvement of women in economic and political decision-making and will be critical to the successful implementation of Agenda 21.

Objectives

24.2 The following objectives are proposed for national Governments:

(a) To implement the Nairobi Forward-looking Strategies for the Advancement of Women, particularly with regard to women's participation in national ecosystem management and control of environment degradation;

(b) to increase the proportion of women decision-makers,

planners, technical advisers, managers and extension workers in environment and development fields;

(c) To consider developing and issuing by the year 2000 a strategy of changes necessary to eliminate constitutional, legal, administrative, cultural, behavioural, social and economic obstacles to women's full participation in sustainable development and in public life;

(d) To establish by the year 1995 mechanisms at the national, regional and international levels to assess the implementation and impact of development and environment policies and programmes on women and to ensure their contributions and benefits;

(e) To assess, review, revise and implement, where appropriate, curricula and other educational material, with a view to promoting the dissemination to both men and women of gender-relevant knowledge and valuation of women's roles through formal and non-formal education, as well as through training institutions, in collaboration with non-governmental organisations;

(f) To formulate and implement clear governmental policies and national guidelines, strategies and plans for the achievement of equality in all aspects of society, including the promotion of women's literacy, education, training, nutrition and health and their participation in key decision-making positions and in management of the environment, particularly as it pertains to their access to resources, by facilitating better access to all forms of credit, particularly in the informal sector, taking measures towards ensuring women's access to property rights as well as agricultural inputs and implements;

(g) To implement, as a matter of urgency, in accordance with country-specific conditions, measures to ensure that women and men have the same right to decide freely and responsibly the number and spacing of their children and have access to information, education and means, as appropriate, to enable them to exercise this right in keeping with their freedom, dignity and personally held values;

(h) To consider adopting, strengthening and enforcing legislation prohibiting violence against women and to take all necessary administrative, social and educational measures to eliminate violence against women in all its forms.

Activities

24.3. Governments should take active steps to implement the following:

(a) Measures to review policies and establish plans to increase the proportion of women involved as decision-makers, planners, managers, scientists and technical advisers in the design, development and implementation of policies and programmes for sustainable development;

(b) Measures to strengthen and empower women's bureaux, women's non-governmental organisations and women's groups in enhancing capacity-building for sustainable development;

(c) Measures to eliminate illiteracy among females and to expand the enrolment of women and girls in educational institutions, to promote the goal of universal access to primary and secondary education for girl children and for women, and to increase educational and training opportunities for women and girls in sciences and technology, particularly at the post-secondary level;

(d) Programmes to promote the reduction of the heavy workload of women and girl children at home and outside through the establishment of more and affordable nurseries and kindergartens by Governments, local authorities, employers and other relevant organisations and the sharing of household tasks by men and women on an equal basis, and to promote the provision of environmentally sound technologies which have been designed, developed and improved in consultation with women, accessible and clean water, an efficient fuel supply and adequate sanitation facilities;

(e) Programmes to establish and strengthen preventive and curative health facilities, which include women-centered, women-managed, safe and effective reproductive health care and affordable, accessible, responsible planning of family size and services, as appropriate, in keeping with freedom, dignity and personally held values. Programmes should focus on providing comprehensive health care, including pre-natal care, education and information on health and responsible parenthood, and should provide the opportunity for all women to fully breastfeed at least during the first four months post-partum. Programmes should fully support women's productive and reproductive roles and well-being and should pay special attention to the need to provide equal and improved health care for all children and to reduce the risk of maternal and child mortality and sickness;

(f) Programmes to support and strengthen equal employment opportunities and equitable remuneration for women in the formal and informal sectors with adequate economic, political and social support systems and services, including child care, particularly day-care facilities and parental leave, and equal access to credit, land and other natural resources;

(g) Programmes to establish rural banking systems with a view to facilitating and increasing rural women's access to credit and to agricultural inputs and implements;

(h) Programmes to develop consumer awareness and the active participation of women, emphasising their crucial role in achieving changes necessary to reduce or eliminate unsustainable patterns of consumption and production, particularly in industrialised countries, in order to encourage investment in environmentally sound productive activities and induce environmentally and socially friendly industrial development;

(i) Programmes to eliminate persistent negative images, stereotypes, attitudes and prejudices against women through changes in socialisation patterns, the media, advertising, and formal and non-formal education;

(j) Measures to review progress made in these areas, including the preparation of a review and appraisal report which includes recommendations to be submitted to the 1995 world conference on women.

24.4. Governments are urged to ratify all relevant conventions pertaining to women if they have not already done so. Those that have ratified conventions should enforce and establish legal, constitutional and administrative procedures to transform agreed rights into domestic legislation and should adopt measures to implement them in order to strengthen the legal capacity of women for full and equal participation in issues and decisions on sustainable development.

24.5. States parties to the Convention on the Elimination of All Forms of Discrimination against Women should review and suggest amendments to it by the year 2000, with a view to strengthening those elements of the Convention related to environment and development, giving special attention to the issue of access and entitlements to natural resources, technology, creative banking facilities and low-cost housing, and the control of pollution and toxicity in the home and workplace. States parties should also clarify the extent of the Conventions' scope with respect to the issues of environment and development and request the Committee on the Elimination of Discrimination against Women to develop guidelines regarding the nature of reporting such issues, required under particular articles of the Convention.

Areas Requiring Urgent Action

24.6. Countries should take urgent measures to avert the ongoing rapid environmental and economic degradation in developing countries that generally affects the lives of women and children in rural areas suffering drought, desertification and deforestation, armed hostilities, natural disasters, toxic waste and the aftermath of the use of unsuitable agro-chemical products.

24.7. In order to reach these goals, women should be fully involved in decision-making and in the implementation of sustainable development activities.

Research, Data Collection and Dissemination of Information

24.8. Countries should develop gender-sensitive

databases, information systems and participatory action-oriented research and policy analyse with the collaboration of academic institutions and local women researchers on the following:

(a) Knowledge and experience on the part of women of the management and conservation of natural resources for incorporation in the databases and information systems for sustainable development;

(b) The impact of structural adjustment programmes on women. In research done on structural adjustment programmes, special attention should be given to the differential impact of those programmes on women, especially in terms of cut-backs in social services, education and health and in the removal of subsidies on food and fuel;

(c) The impact on women of environmental degradation, particularly drought, desertification, toxic chemicals and armed hostilities;

(d) Analysis of the structural linkages between gender relations, environment and development;

(e) The integration of the value of unpaid work, including work that is currently designated "domestic", in resource accounting mechanisms in order to better represent the true value of the contribution of women to the economy, using revised guidelines for the United Nations System of National Accounts, to be issued in 1993;

(f) Measures to develop and include environmental, social gender impact analysis as an essential step in the development and monitoring of programmes and policies;

(g) Programmes the create rural and urban training, research and resource centres in developing and developed countries that will serve to disseminate environmentally sound technologies to women.

International and Regional Cooperation and Coordination

24.9. The Secretary-General of the United Nations should review the adequacy of all United Nations institutions, including those with a special focus on the role of women, in meeting development and environment objectives, and make recommendations for strengthening their capacities. Institutions that require special attention in this area include the Division for the Advancement of Women (Centre for Social Development and Humanitarian Affairs, United Nations Office at Vienna), the United Nations Development Fund for Women (UNIFEM), the International Research and Training Institute for the Advancement of Women (INSTRAW) and the women's programmes of regional commissions. The review should consider how the environment and development programmes of each body of the United Nations system could be strengthened to implement Agenda 21 and how to incorporate the role of women in programmes and decisions related to sustainable development.

24.10. Each body of the United Nations system should review the number of women in senior policy-level and decision-making posts and, where appropriate, adopt programmes to increase that number, in accordance with Economic and Social Council resolution 1991/17 on the improvement of the status of women in the Secretariat.

24.11. UNIFEM should establish regular consultations with donors in collaboration with UNICEF, with a view to promoting operational programmes and projects on sustainable development that will strengthen the participation of women, especially low-income women, in sustainable development and in decision-making. UNDP should establish a women's focal point on development and environment in each of its resident representative offices to provide information and promote exchange of experience and information in these fields. Bodies of the United Nations system, governments and non-governmental organisations involved in the follow-up to the Conference and the implementation of Agenda 21 should ensure that gender considerations are fully integrated into all the policies, programmes and activities.

MEANS OF IMPLEMENTATION

Finance and Cost Evaluation

24.12. The UNCED Secretariat has estimated the average total annual cost (1993-2000) of implementing the activities of this chapter to be about $40 million from the international community on grant and concessional terms. These are indicative and order of magnitude estimates only and have not been reviewed by governments. Actual costs and financial terms, including any that are non-concessional, will depend upon, *inter alia,* the specific strategies and programmes governments decide upon for implementation.

TREATY ON ENVIRONMENTAL EDUCATION FOR SUSTAINABLE SOCIETIES AND GLOBAL RESPONSIBILITY

(This treaty, as in education, is a dynamic process and should therefore promote reflection, debate and amendments.)

We signatories, people from all part of the globe, are devoted to protecting life on earth and recognise the central role of education in shaping values and social action. We commit ourselves to a process of educational transformation aimed at involving ourselves, our communities and nations in creating equitable and sustainable societies. In so doing we seek to bring new hope to our small, troubled, but still beautiful planet.

Introduction

We consider that environmental education for equitable sustainability is a continuous learning process based on respect for all life. Such education affirms values and actions which contribute to human and social transformation and ecological preservation. It fosters ecologically sound and equitable societies that live together in interdependence and diversity. This requires individual and collective responsibility at local, national and planetary level.

We consider that preparing ourselves for the required changed depends on advancing collective understanding of the systemic nature of the crises that threaten the world's future. The root causes of such problems as increasing poverty, environmental deterioration and communal violence can be found in the dominant socio-economic system. This system is based on over-production and over-consumption for some and under-consumption and indequate conditions to produce for the great majority.

We consider that inherent in the crisis are an erosion of basic values and the alienation and non-participation of almost all individuals in the building of their own future. It is of fundamental importance that the world's communities design and work out their own alternatives to existing policies. Such alternatives include the abolition of those programmes of development, adjustment and economic reform which maintain the existing growth model with its devastating effects on the environment and its diverse species, including the human one.

We consider that environmental education should urgently bring about change in the quality of life and a greater consciousness of personal conduct, as well as harmony among human beings and between them and other forms of life.

Some Principles of Environmental Education for Equitable and Sustainable Societies

1. Education is the right of all; we are all learners and educators.
2. Environmental education, whether formal, non-formal or informal, should be grounded in critical and innovative thinking in any place or time, promoting the transformation and construction of society.
3. Environmental education is both individual and collective. It aims to develop local and global citizenship with respect for self-determination and the sovereignty of nations.
4. Environmental education is not neutral but is value based. It is an act for social transformation.
5. Environmental education must involve a holistic approach and thus an interdisciplinary focus in the relation between human beings, nature and the universe.
6. Environmental education must stimulate solidarity, equality, and respect for human rights involving democratic strategies and an open climate of cultural interchange.
7. Environmental education should treat critical global issues, their causes and interrelationships in a systemic approach and within their social and historical contexts. Fundamental issues in relation to development and the environment, such as

population, health, peace, human rights, democracy, hunger, degradation of flora and fauna, should be perceived in this manner.

8. Environmental education must facilitate equal partnerships in the processes of decision-making at all levels and stages.
9. Environmental education must recover, recognise, respect, reflect and utilise indigenous history and local cultures, as well as promote cultural, linguistic and ecological diversity. This implies acknowledging the historical perspective of native peoples as a way to change ethnocentric approaches, as well as the encouragement of bilingual education.
10. Environmental education should empower all peoples and promote opportunities for grassroots democratic change and participation. This means that communities must region control of their own destiny.
11. Environmental education values all different forms of knowledge. Knowledge is diverse, cumulative and socially produced and should not be patented or monopolised.
12. Environmental education must be designed to enable people to manage conflicts in just and humane ways.
13. Environmental education must stimulate dialogue and cooperation among individuals and institutions in order to create new lifestyles which are based on meeting everyone's basic needs, regardless of ethnic, gender, age, religious, class physical or mental differences.
14. Environmental education require a democratisation of the mass media and its commitment to the interests of all sectors of society. Communication

is an inalienable right and the mass media must be transformed into one of the main channels of education, not only by disseminating information on an egalitarian basis, but also through the exchange of means, values and experiences.

15. Environmental education must integrate knowledge, skills, values, attitudes and actions. It should convert every opportunity into an educational experience for sustainable societies.
16. Education must help develop an ethical awareness of all forms of life with which humans share this planet, respect all life cycles and impose limits on human's exploitation of other forms of life.

Plan of Action

The organisation that sign this Treaty will implement policies to:

1. Turn the declarations of this Treaty and of other Treaties produced by the Conference of Citizens' Groups during the RIO 92 process into documents for use in formal education systems and in education programmes of social movements and social organisations.
2. Work on environmental education for sustainable societies together with groups that draft other Treaties approved during RIO 92.
3. Make comparative studies of the treaties of citizens' groups and those produced by the United Nations Conference on Environment and Development (UNCED) and use the conclusions in educational activities.
4. Work on the principles of this Treaty from the perspective of local situations, necessarily relating

them to the state of the planet, creating a consciousness for transformation.

5. Promote knowledge, policies, methods, and practices in all areas of formal, informal and non-formal environmental education and for all age groups.
6. Promote and support training for environmental conservation, preservation and management, as part of the exercise of local and planetary citizenship.
7. Encourage individuals and groups to take positions, and institutions to make policies, that constantly review the coherence between what is said and what is done, as well as the values of our cultures, traditions and history
8. Circulate information about people's wisdom and memory, and support and inform about appropriate initiatives and technologies in relation to the use of natural resources.
9. Promote gender co-responsibility in relation to production, reproduction and the maintenance of life.
10. Stimulate and support the creation and strengthening of ecologically responsible producers' and consumers' associations, and commercial networks, that provide ecologically sound alternatives.
11. Sensitise populations so that they establish People's Councils for Environmental Management and Ecological Action to research, discuss, inform and decide on environmental problems and policies.
12. Create educational, judicial, organisational and political conditions to guarantee that governments allocate a significant part of their budgets to education and the environment.

13. Promote partnership and cooperation among NGOs, social movements, and the UN agencies (UNESCO, UNEP, FAO and others) at national, regional and international levels to jointly set priorities for action in education, environment and development.
14. Promote the creation and strengthening of national, regional and international networks for joint action between organisations of the South, North, East and West with a planetary perspective (e.g. foreign debt, human rights, peace, global warming, population, contaminated products).
15. Ensure that the media becomes an educational instrument for the preservation and conservation of natural resources presenting a plurality of views and reliable and contextualised information; and stimulate the broadcasting of programmes generated by local communities.
16. Promote an understanding of the causes of consumerist behaviour and act to change practices and the systems that maintain them.
17. Search for self-managed, economically and ecologically appropriate alternatives of production which contribute to an improvement in the quality of life.
18. Act to eradicate sexist, racist and any other prejudices, as well as contribute to the promotion of cultural diversity, territorial rights and self-determination.
19. Mobilise formal and non-formal institutions of higher education in support of teaching, research and extension towards the community in environmental education, and the creation in each University of interdisciplinary centres for the environment.

20. Strengthen social organisations and movements in order to enhance the exercise of citizenship and an improvement in the quality of life and the environment.
21. Assure that ecological organisations popularise their activities and that communities incorporate ecological issues in everyday life.
22. Establish criteria for the approval of education projects for sustainable societies, discussing social priorities with funding agencies.

Coordination, Monitoring and Evaluation Systems

All signatories of the Treaty agree to:

1. Distribute and promote tho Treaty on Environmental Education for Sustainable Societies and Global Responsibility in all countries, through joint campaigns by NGOs, social movements and others.
2. Stimulate and create organisations and groups of NGOs and social movements to initiate, implement, follow, and evaluate the elements of this Treaty.
3. Produce materials to publicise this Treaty and its unfolding into educational action, in the form of texts, educational materials courses, research, cultural events, media programmes, fairs of popular creativity, electronic mail, and other means.
4. Form an international coordination group to give continuity to the proposals in this treaty.
5. Stimulate, create and develop networks of environmental educators.
6. Ensure the 1st Planetary Meeting of Environmental Education for Sustainable Societies is held within three years.

7. Coordinate action to support social movements which are working for improving the quality of life, extending effective international solidarity.
8. Foster links between NGOs and social movements to review their strategies and programmes on environment and education.

Groups to be Involved

This Treaty is aimed at:

1. Organisations of social movements—ecologist, women's, youth, ethnic, farmers', union, neighbourhood and artistic groups and others.
2. NGOs committed to grassroots social movements.
3. Professional educators interested in establishing programmes related to environmental issues in formal education systems and other educational activities.
4. Those responsible for the mass media who are ready to accept the challenge of openness and democracy, thus initiating a new concept of mass communication.
5. Scientists and scientific institutions that take ethical positions and are sympathetic to the work of social movements and organisations.
6. Religious groups interested in working with social organisations and movements.
7. Local and national governments able to act in tune and in partnership with the aims of this Treaty.
8. Business people committed to working within a rationale of recovery, conservation and improvement of the environment and the quality of life.
9. Alternative communities that experience new

lifestyles in harmony with the principles and aims of this Treaty.

Resources

All signatories of this Treaty are committed to:

1. Allocating a significant part of their resources to the development of educational programmes related to an improvement of the environment and quality of life.
2. Demanding that governments allocate a significant percentage of Gross National Product to supporting programmes of environmental education in all sectors of public administration, with the direct participation of NGOs and social movements.
3. Propose economic policies that stimulate business to develop and apply appropriate technology and create environmental education programmes for the community, and as part of personnel training.
4. Encouraging funding agencies to prioritise and allocate significant resources to environmental education and ensure its presence in projects they approve wherever possible.
5. Contributing to the formation of a cooperative and decentralised global banking system for NGOs and social movements that will use part of its resources for educational programmes and at the same time be an exemplary exercise in using financial resources.

Members of the NGOs Working Group of the Treaty on Environmental Education for Sustainable Societies and Global Responsibility were:

Coordination

Moema Viezzet	—	ICAE, Brazil
Joelle Danant	—	AFGE, USA
Marcos Sorrentino	—	SODEMAP, Brazil
Marta Benavides	—	MEDEPAZ, El Salvador
Marta Simons	—	SAAE, Brazil
Nigel Hartley	—	SUM, Switzerland
Omar Ovalles	—	Habitat, Venezuela
Rachel Trajber	—	FED, Brazil

Collaborators:

Arab States	—	ALECSO, Tunisia
Africa	—	AALAE, Kenya
North America	—	FES, Canada
Latin America	—	CEAAL, Chile
Asia	—	ASPBAE, Macau
Europe	—	DCAE, Denmark
	—	WUS Germany
The Caribbean	—	CARCAE, Jamaica

Finally, with this text, we have the version of the Treaty on Environmental Education for Sustainable Societies and Global Responsibility, whose aim is to elicit the commitment of all active and interested people to a series of principles.

The process that led to the elaboration of this Treaty can be described in the following stages:

1. The elaboration of a Charter on Environmental Education in four languages, with the subsequent collection and systematisation of comments improving and modifying it from five continents between August 1991 and March 1992.

2. In March 1992 the then Charter on Environmental Education was introduced at the 4th Preparatory Committee (PrepCom) in New York where it was reelaborated by the NGO Education Working Group, which expanded it not only in terms of its concepts but also in its format and the composition of the group responsible for its development. It thus took on the characteristics of a Treaty, an international agreement to be signed by individuals and organisations concerned with education.

Guidelines were given by the NGO Coordination Group for UNCED for the elaboration of documents that contained: An Introduction, Principles, A Plan of Action, Coordination and Monitoring Mechanisms, Groups to be Involved, and Resources. The first two sections were discussed in New York.

3. In April/May 1992 the texts elaborated in New York were once again circulated internationally, thereby completing the drafts of the other four sections.

Finally this text was translated into four languages and printed for discussion in the Journey on Environmental Education in the context of Rio/92.

4. During the Journey in June 1992 a last stage in the elaboration of the text led to a final version after 14 hours of discussion in plenary sessions and workshops, and many hours of incorporating and editing the additional proposals into the text. This version was then translated into the four languages adopted by the International NGO Forum.

The official launch of the Treaty took place on 7 June 1992, during an Eco-Carnival Parade with the participation of 2000 children from the Samba School Flowers for Tomorrow, Brazil.

On 9 June the Treaty was presented to the plenary session of the international NGO Forum, after which a group met to discuss specific points which still required consensus. Some additional comments were made in the plenary and are included in an annex, reflecting the start of a new stage of implementing the Treaty which began in Rio. The process then also started to collect the signatures of those supporting and committed to the implementation of the Treaty.

5. Two plenaries on 11 and 13 June will complete this process, deciding collectively possible forms of coordination and monitoring in relation to the Treaty's implementation.

This act, unique in the history of civil society, shows commitment to change, and at the same time a demand that governments change.

Rio de Janeiro, 9th June 1992

Bibliography

Alan Maynard, Welfare, who pays? Philip Bean ed. *In Defence of Welfare* (London, Tavistock Publication, 1985) p. 142.

Anne Minahan, "Purpose and Objectives of Social Work Revisted" *Social Work,* 26:1 (Jan. 1931) p. 6.

Armando Morales and Bradford, Sheafor *Social Work A Profession of Many Faces,* 5th edition (**Boston:** Allyn and Bacon, 1989) p. 7.

Belly Baer and Ronald Federico, *Educating The Baccalaureate Social Workers* (Ballinger. Cambridge. 1975) p. 61.

Betty J Piccard, *An Introduction to Social Work* (Illinious: Dorsay Press, 1983) p. 45-46.

Eugene Pusic, *Reappraisal of the United Nations Social Programmes,* (New York, 1965).

Gore M.S. 1981: The Scope of Social work Practice" in T.K. Nair (ed.), Social Work Education and Social Work Practices in India Madras, Association of Schools of Schools of Social Work in India.

H. Kumar, *Social work An Experience and Experiment in India* p. 83.

Halmos, P. 1978: *The Personal and the Political,* London, Hutchinson.

Hans Nagpaul, *Culture, Education, and Social Welfare, Need for Indigenous Foundations,* (New Delhi, S. Chand, 1979).

Harry Specht, *New Directions for Social Work Practice,* (New Jersey, Printice Hall, , 1938) p. 4.

Helen Wright, "Similarities and Differences in Social Work Education as Seen in India and North America," *International Social Work,* January, 1959.

Herbert Aptaker, "Social Work in Cross Cultural Perspective;" in S.K. Khinduka (ed.) Social *Work in India,* (Allahabad, 1965).

Jackson C Eugene, Macy J. Harry Day J. Phyllis 1984: *"A Simultaneity Model for Social Work Education".*

K.S. Mandal, "American Influence on Social Work Education in India and its Impact", *International Social Work,* 1989, Vol. 32; also see, Krishnan Nair (ed.). *Social Work Education and Social Work Practice in India,* op.cit.

Krishnan Nair, T. (ed.) *Social Work Education and Social Work Practice in India,* (Madras, Association of Schools of Social Work in India, 1981).

Kulkarni, P.D. 1979: *Social Policy and Social Development in India,* Madras, Association of Schools of Social Work in India.

Lee James Midgley, *Professional Imperialism* (London, Heinemann, 1981). No Western scholar has ever written such a forceful critique of American social work and its global diffusion.

M.S. Gore, "The Scope of Social Work Practice" Krishan Nair (ed.) *Social Work Education and Social Work Practice in India,* (Madras, Association of School of Social work in India 1981) p. 9.

Mans Shardt, Clifford 1971: "Education for Social Work," *Indian Journal of Social Work.* Vol. II, No.1.

Morales and Sheafar, *Social Work a Profession of Many Faces* 5th ed. p. 125.

Nafisa D'Souza 1984: *Social work Education:- A Prospective for Social Change,* Mumbai Mimeographed.

Nitto Neece, *Social Work,* (New Jersey, Printice Hall, 1990), p. 7.

Pathak Shankar 1981: *Social Welfare,* Delhi. MacMillan India Ltd.

Pathak, S.H., "Social Development and Social Work - Some Unsolved Issues" Nayak and Siddiqui (ed) *Social Work and Social Development* (New Delhi, Gitanjali Publication, 1989) pp. 7-8.

Pincus, A. & Minahan, Anne 1973: *Social Work Practice: Model and Method.* Ithaca: Peacock Publishers.

Rex. A, Skidmore and others, *"Introduction to Social Work"* (New Jessey, Printice Hall, 1991) p. 19.

Siddiqui H.Y. (ed) 1984: *Social Work and Social Action,* New Delhi, Harnam Publication.

Skidmore and others. *Introduction to Social Work,* p. 13.

Titus P.M. 1941: The Place of Research in Social Work" *Indian Journal of Social Work,* Vol. 11, No.1.

Turner, F.J. 1974: *Social Treatment.* New York. The Free Press.

Warner. W. Boehm, *Objectives of The Social Work Curriculum in the Future Curriculum Study* 1. (New York, Council on Social Work Education. 1959) p. 54.

Wilensky and Lebeaux, *Industrial Society and Social Welfare,* New York, Free Press 1965), p. 138 quoted by Pothak, Social Welfare, p. 159-160.

Wilson, Elizabeth 1977: *Women and the Welfare State,* London, Tavistock Publication.

Index

A

Adolescent Girls, 252
American Social Work Education, 162
AMHP, 2
Andhra Pradesh, 261
ASW, 2
Australia, 117
Austria, 122

B

Bangladesh, 118
BAOM, 113
BIS, 111
BLA, 112
Bombay Cooperative Credit Societies Act of 1925, 210
Brazil, 272
BSET, 109
BSGS, 112
BSPH, 115

C

Canada, 101
Career in Social Work Education, 100
Chennai, 166
Child survival, 50
China, 118
Clifford Manshardt, 26
Cold War, 21
Columbia University School of Social Work, 161
Community organisation, 50
Criminal Justice, 55
CSWE, 131
CSWI, 189

D

Denmark, 122
Drug addict, 50
DSW, 2, 129

E

Educated Unemployment, 151
Education Commission (1966), 85
Education for Social Work, 5
Employment Services, 55
Environmental education, 272

F

Factories Act 1948, 193

Family,
  planning, 55
  welfare, 65
France, 123

G

Gandhiji, 96
Girl Child, 256
Global Action for Women, 261
Gore, 34
GSCC, 2
Gujarat, 260

H

Halmos, 33
Harriett Barlett, 37
Haryana, 260
Higher education, 131, 135, 147
Hong Kong, 100

I

IASSW, 130
India, 119
Indian Council for Child Welfare, 64
Indian higher education, 179
Indian schools of social work, 168
Indian social scientists, 90
Indian social work, 90, 165
  education, 163
Indigenous thought, 183
Indira Gandhi, 189
International Social Work, 56
Italy, 124

J

Jackson, 31
Japan, 119

K

Karnataka, 261
Kerala, 261
Kolkatta, 166
Kulkarni, 31

L

Labour,
  Bureau, 215
  Legislation, 193
LLB, 116

M

Madhya Pradesh, 260
Maharashtra, 260
Margaret Alva, 190
Mass communication, 272
Mental Health Act 1983, 2
MSW, 129
Multiple Social Work, 88
Mumbai, 166

N

National Commission of Labour, 213
National Plan of Action on Children, 217
Netherlands, 124
New Zealand, 100, 119
NPPW, 190

P

Pakistan, 120
Pathak, S.H., 41
Personality disorders, 10
Philippines, 121
Professional,
  education, 3
  organisations, 59
  social work, 92
  social workers, 54
Protestant Ethic, 159
Public Welfare, 55, 95

R

Rajasthan, 260
Report of the Education Commission, 145

S

SAARC, 219
Seargent Report, 138
Shram Shakti, 191
Slum improvement, 50
Social,
  service, 89
  welfare, 22
    activities, 52
  Work, 37, 78, 87, 92
    assistance, 41
    education, 1, 7, 11, 18, 26, 131, 178
    intervention, 44
    literature, 175
    periodicals, 177
    practice, 37
    profession, 54
    services, 44
    tasks, 28
    workers, 2
Sri Lanka, 122
Switzerland, 127

T

Tamil Nadu, 261
Tata Institute, 8
The Minimum Wages Act, 1948, 204
Tribal welfare, 81

U

UNCED, 272
United Kingdom, 2
United Nations, 180
  Survey, 181
University Education Commission, 85
USA, 104, 272

V

Vivek, 213

W

West Bengal, 260
Western concepts, 186
Wilson, 87
World War II, 162

Y

YWCA, 3

■■■